Mabel!

Mabel!

A Once in a lifetime,
West Coast Travel Adventure

---

by Everett L. Jennings
& Jon C. Rogers

Dedication

This book is dedicated to

Everett Jennings
and Clark Baldwin

and to all those who understand

Life is not the destination,

Life is the Journey.

Contents

Did This Really Happen?

This is a true story based on journals, notes, photographs and interviews made at the time. It is told mostly from the point of view of Everett Jennings who was inspired to write the original draft immediately upon our return. Before his passing, I promised him I would complete our story and see it published.

Here you are, Ev.

To assist the modern traveler, I've updated the original story to include more current details and Website addresses about the unusual places we discovered.

The events and conversations are largely as recorded at the time; the opinions are those of the speakers. Of the real people described, some have passed away. Information has been omitted to protect those still living.

Of course, much has changed since our original voyage. I have tried to indicate these changes. If the reader wishes to retrace the roads described in the story and re-discover these unique places as they exist today, they should be aware of this.

Think of this as a true life adventure, and an example of what the unknown realm of reality might have in store for you.

Jon C. Rogers
The Mainland
2020

Our first sign of danger was the smoke.

It crept up the sky from the south and slowly began blocking out the sun. Brush fires began popping up alongside the highway. Then, directly up in front of us, the forest burst into a blazing inferno. Suddenly, the world had become a smoky hell, filled with fiery, red and orange flames.

What am I doing here? Here I am, dressed in plain clothes, riding in an open roadster—no fire protection at all—driving straight into a raging forest fire? This is nuts.

How did I get into this? Wasn't I just coming home from a wonderful, week-long summer vacation? Was it really only last week I was safe at home—as snug as a bug in a rug—asleep in my bed?

1 – Wake Up! Call to Action!

The soft gentle ringing of the telephone brought me slowly out of my deep sleep. It was 5 a.m., Saturday, August 29th, 1987. I knew it was Jon. He is my closest friend of more than twenty years, and this was his wakeup call at my apartment in Belmont, California. I gathered my thoughts, cleared my head, picked up the phone and spoke in my most articulate tongue.

"Hwoolggg."

"Everett, is that you?" Jon's voice came from the receiver.

I said, "Surg ig me, wass matgrr."

"Hey Everett, wake up! I'm picking you up in half an hour, okay?"

"Okeg," I replied and hung up.

(I don't know how he can talk at five in the morning.) Slowly…very slowly…I crawled out of bed.

This morning, Jon and I are starting a long planned, sight-seeing vacation trip to his hometown in faraway Washington State.

Years ago, I had taken Jon to my home town of Stockton, California. And for a long time, Jon had said he wanted to take me on a grand tour on all the back roads of the West Coast to his home town. So, after years of anticipation, it's payback time.

Our transportation will be "Mabel." Mabel is Jon's 1955 Jaguar Roadster which he has been quickly restoring over the last twenty years. (He told me once, "Take it slow, it takes longer if you hurry!")

Privately, I am still a little apprehensive about making such a long trip in a car that is over 30 years old, restored or not. (That was then. Mabel is now over 60. Shhh! Don't tell her! She thinks she's still young. JR)

There is going to be a shortage of parts if we break down. There is going to be a lack of space in the little car for my 220 pound, 5'-9" frame. There will also be a lack of space to carry back any treasures we might find along the way. It seems to me we will be lacking a lot.

However, I agreed to the trip because I have faith in Jon's ability to repair anything that Mabel might break. Also, I figured if I get too cramped, there are big busses and fast planes. And if I find a treasure I just have to have; I can rent a trailer. I know Jon won't mind me hitching a dirty, dented, faded-orange Rent-A-Trailer to the back of his sleek, elegant, eye-catching roadster. Noooo, not a bit.

Our plan is to drive north on Interstate 5 to Redding, turn west on 299 to the little town of Weaverville where we'll meet up with our old friend Clark. He will be adventuring north with us on "Moonshadow" his Honda Gold Wing. We'll have a motorcycle escort all the way!

From Weaverville we will travel the back roads through the Trinity Alps, cross over to Weed, and then drive up Highway 97 through inland Oregon and Washington. Up near the Canadian border, we'll cross over the Cascade Mountains to the coast. There we'll visit Canada, the Olympic Peninsula and the San Juan islands, before turning for home. On our way back, we'll stop at Portland to participate in the All British Field Meet and then shoot for home on I-5. It should be a nice, relaxing, sight-filled, one week vacation tour of some of the most unusual places on the West Coast.

(Had I known what was really in store for us, I probably wouldn't have gone.)

About forty-five minutes later, Jon arrived as planned. We're both excited. Mabel looks beautiful in her deep maroon paint, chrome wire wheels and shiny accessories. The deep throated rumbling from her dual overhead cam, six-cylinder engine, is music to my ears.

I had already packed the night before so all we have to do is load up and go. The boot (the "trunk" to us Yanks), is small but our limited luggage fits. I suggest adding some extra gear, including a water jug and an ice cooler. Jon is skeptical at first but with some adjusting, we manage to wedge them behind the passenger's seat.

At last we're ready. We climb in and click on the lap straps (That's the English term for seat belts. You know, we *are* in an English car, and we *must* be proper). Jon turns the key, hits the starter button and Mabel roars to life. Little thrills race through me.

At last this is really happening. Jon releases the emergency brake, shifts into low, eases out the clutch, and we motor slowly off down the street in the early, pre-dawn glow.

We are on our way.

2 – Dawn Patrol: Into The Valley

The sun hasn't quite peeped over the mountains in the east bay as we rumble through the empty city. Shifting smoothly through the gears, Jon carefully guides Mabel through the sleepy streets. We stop at Chucks Donuts for two coffees and two buttermilk donuts to go. Carefully sipping our hot coffee and munching on our donuts, we enter onto Highway 101 and turn north. There is very little early morning traffic.

I finish my coffee and donut, push back in the seat and watch as the green hills and gentle blue waters of the San Francisco Bay Area slip past us in the early morning glow of the rising sun.

Off to the West side I can see morning fog. It is lying softly on the landscape. It reminds me of paintings I saw in Japan so long, long ago. My thoughts wander back to my life in Japan. That had been a good time.

As we continue cruising up the highway, the early morning air starts knifing through me. I am getting cold. I grab my extra sweater, pull on my wind breaker, and turn up the heater to high. After a few minutes I warm back up and start to enjoy the ride.

We're passing through San Francisco now. The ghostly outlines of skyscrapers peek through the fog as it drifts slowly across the city. As we start up over the Bay Bridge the fog lifts slightly and the morning sun casts a golden glow on the calm bay waters below.

Jon loads our first tape into the stereo. The music of *Top Gun* comes booming out of well-hidden stereo speakers in Mabel's open cockpit. Looking up, I see nearby clouds passing close overhead. Looking down off the bridge, far below are the dark blue waters of the bay. The music, the sky and the wind whipping past my head gives me the feeling we are flying. It is like we're soaring high in the sky, spreading our wings to the morning sun.

Suddenly, our car's open cockpit becomes that of an ancient biplane. I get the feeling it is the morning of April 21, 1918. We're in a Sopwith Camel with twin Vickers machine guns. Jon is Captain A. Roy Brown and we are going after Baron Manfred von Richthofen and his red Fokker Dr I Triplane.

"Red Baron! Where are you?"

He is a most gallant and deadly foe, but we are ready. In a moment we will be matching him in a dog fight, wings locked in mortal combat…a duel to the death. A shiver of excitement races through me at the thought. I look at the white, puffy clouds all around us, but no Red

Baron. He must know we are looking for him and has decided to stay out of the skies today. Lucky for him.

Our imaginary flight takes us up, arcing high over the bay at the crest of the bridge and back down to the water's edge on the opposite shore. Ahead the road flattens out, looking like a runway, welcoming us back from the successful sortie of our dawn patrol. So this is what the early pilots had felt like, flying in their open cockpits. To be alone with the sky, the clouds, the wind, and the possibility of death. My shiver turns into a thrill.

As we leave the bridge behind, I am surprised by the little imaginary adventure I've just had. The feeling of flying among the clouds in an ancient biplane had all come from riding in Mabel's small open cockpit with its cut-down doors, surrounded by the music, sunshine, wind and clouds. She had exposed me to my surroundings with such intensity that I was transported to another time and place. I never knew riding in an open roadster could be such a different experience. Amazing.

We turn north on Highway 80 which will take us to Vacaville where we will make the connection to Highway 505.

It is 7:30 a.m. when we cross the Carquiniz Bridge. I look up and watch the steel bridge supports as they flash overhead. They mesmerize and hypnotize me. I get the feeling as though I'm falling in slow motion. Abruptly, the bridge ends and I snap back to reality. Afterwards the image stays with me for a long time. I never knew sensations like this before. Only in an open car is one aware of the amazing world passing above you.

We pass the towns of Vallejo and Fairfield in quick order. As we pass Vacaville, my stomach begins to growl, "Feed Me. Feed Me." But Jon can't hear my stomach's growling. He keeps going up I-505 until we reach Interstate 5. Even when we pass Arbuckle and Williams we press on. I'm having a hard time holding down my hunger. Maybe if I chew on his arm…?

Then I notice Jon seems to be distracted by something. Now it's not a good sign when a guy who's normally a 'motor-mouth' doesn't say anything for quite some time.

"Hey buddy, wha's up?" I inquire.

"Well, after we got out of the Bay area I wanted to give Mabel her head—you know, crank her up a notch or two—so we could make some time." He replies.

"Yea?" I reply. "I didn't notice…we don't seem to be going any faster than before."

"Yes, that's what's got me worried. Mabel doesn't seem to want to go any faster. I'm giving her gas but she's not picking up any speed. She's running ok, but it's like she's pushing against some kind of resistance. I can get her up to about sixty-five and that's all."

Really? And I was having such a good time. "Maybe she's running out of breath?" I venture.

"Huh? I don't think so, Ev. She's got three carburetors. And during her restoration I designed a special four-inch diameter pipe that runs up to the front of the car, under the bumper so they can get pressurized fresh air. My friend Jim put a lot of work into building that intake. I don't see how Mabel could possibly be running out of breath."

"How fast did you say she'll go?" Honestly, I hadn't noticed the problem as we'd been keeping up with traffic. …but then, I wasn't driving.

"She'll go fine up to about sixty but then nothin' after about sixty-five." Jon looks visibly worried. "I just tuned the engine before we left. It's like she's running out of poop. I just don't understand it."

"How long is that intake pipe you added?" I was searching for some clue.

"About three feet," Jon answered. "I have it running into the stock air filter can and then through individual two-inch pipes feeding each carburetor."

We travel along a few more minutes in silence. I am beginning to think about how this feels like a bad omen for the trip. Jon looks like he's deep in thought …at least that is the look in his eyes.

"Naw, it couldn't be," he mutters under his breath, but I hear it well enough to answer, "What?"

But Jon's not answering. He's busy looking at traffic and signaling. Now, he's pulling over to the side of the road. "What?" I ask again, more stridently.

"I've got an idea. I want to test something. You stay here." Jon is up and out of the car. He's running around to my side of the car and, now he's lying down under the right front fender. He's fooling with something. When he gets back up, he has a black metal disk in his hand.

Running back around, he jumps back in, throws the part behind the driver's seat and, checking traffic, sends Mabel charging back onto the freeway.

"What is going on?" I ask as he shifts through the gears, bringing Mabel back up to cruising speed.

"Just a minute and I'll tell ya," he replies. There's an empty road ahead, and he gives Mabel 'the gun.' Mabel responds with a leap forward. Before we know it, we're doing ninety and Jon eases back off the throttle. "Mabel's all better now." He's grinning.

"What did you do?" I ask incredulously, amazed at the instant change in Mabel's performance.

"You were right. I just took the maintenance cover off the air filter." He shouts over the air stream. "It's an access cover that allows me to easily change the filter. Taking it off allowed a second opening for more air to get into the filter. That removed the restriction my "beautifully designed" intake pipe was creating. Bad design. So much for my clean-air theory!"

"Oh." I wonder how a guy can be dumb enough to outsmart himself—and then smart enough to quick fix it.

As we drive farther, I start to relax again. I'd forgotten all about my hunger. Occasionally, I hear Jon muttering under his breath. "But my calculations were right!" I ignore him and turn my attention to the passing scenery.

It is now about 8:30 a.m. and a beautiful morning. Twin hills start to appear to the east of us, on our right. They are the strange and mysterious "Sutter Buttes." They are the only mountains in this enormous flat valley.

Covering an area ten miles in diameter, Sutter Buttes rise about 2,000 feet above the flat farmland. I know that trying to find an entrance to Sutter Buttes either ends up at locked gates or at dead ends on range land with signs threatening legal action. Although it is now private land, once, Native Americans of the Maidu tribe lived there.

They probably thrived on fish, small game and a profusion of nuts and seeds.

Now, Golden Eagles live high on the craggy peaks and soar on thermal currents rising from the hot valley floor below. They fly around looking for small game, while keeping a guarded eye on the sheer bluffs where their nests are hidden. Inside the nests, baby Eagle mouths open and close, making cheeping sounds ("Feed me, feed me"?). I know just how they must feel. Below them, coyote, deer and other small animals frolic on grassy hillsides and green meadows. Shade is found lying under groves of blue oaks. We speed northward, hoping someday to find a way to explore the mysterious Sutter's Buttes[1].

Finally, about 9 a.m., we stop in Willows at a local Denny's for a long overdue breakfast.

Jon has one of his favorites, Eggs Benedict, and I go for the Southern Breakfast; Eggs, Bacon, and biscuits. My empty stomach makes the food taste much better than usual. Now that we're both feeling better, our travel adventure feels like it's really started.

After breakfast, Jon turns to me, "Ok Ev, now that you've got a full stomach and aren't grumbling; I need your help with a little task."

"What's that?" I'm in a good mood so this doesn't sound too bad.

---

[1] See www.parks.ca.gov/?page_id=23786 for more information about a pending future State Park there.

"Well, did you notice that during the drive up here Mabel's ammeter gauge was showing about a fifteen amp charge?"

"No, not really." I honestly hadn't paid attention.

"I didn't want to worry you with it. At first, I thought it was just the battery charging after she's been sitting for so long. But after several hours on the road, there's no way that battery's not charged." He goes on, "I just need a little help in adjusting the regulator. I don't want to burn up the battery by overcharging it."

Hmmm, this sounds a little unusual. But I certainly don't want him to burn up the battery either. "What do you need me to do?"

Jon and I are in the back of the parking lot. "I'll tell you in a minute." He opens up Mabel's trunk (Boot? I always get confused.) and pulls out a special bag. He fishes out a huge manual, a voltmeter and some tools. He then lays a large towel over Mabel's passenger side front fender. Then he bends over the fender and sticks his head deep into the engine compartment.

Sure enough, just about then, people start showing up. They're standing around admiring Mabel. I'm busy answering their questions when I hear a muffled voice from under the hood (Bonnet?).

"Hey EV, climb in, start the engine and rev it up a little. About two thousand RPM will do."

"Are you going to be ok?" I ask as I climb into Mabel's driver's seat. "I'm fine. Go ahead and start her." comes his muffled reply.

I feel somewhat strange, sitting there in Denney's parking lot, in a beautifully restored roadster with a group of spectators watching. I'm racing the engine while my friend is shouting instructions at me with his butt hanging out over the fender. We must be some kind of a sight.

"Ok, how's the ammeter reading now?" Jon shouts over Mabel's roar.

"It's down to about five amps," I shout back.

"How about now?" comes the next question.

"Now it's about two amps," I shout back.

Jon pulls his head out and gives me the signal to cut off the engine. "Ok, it's adjusted now."

Ok, if he thinks it's fine, I'm thinking it's fine. I'm just wondering what all those people are thinking.

Jon gathers up his tools and manual and loads them back into the boot. (There, I said it right.)

He slides into the passenger's seat.

"Ok, Ev, your turn to drive."

"Sure." I fire Mabel back up and we idle out of the parking lot leaving a large group of amazed spectators behind. I guess they're not used to people doing maintenance adjustments on cars in a restaurant parking lot. Heck, we did it all the time when I was a kid.

Since I'm behind the wheel, it's time to get familiar with driving Mabel. At first she doesn't seem too different. Her steering is firm, but her response is very quick. It is a nice morning and the freeway is a straight road. At speed, she's very stable. She even seems to sense the road and track it quite well. This is good. I really don't want to learn how to drive her in a thundering rainstorm on some twisty mountain pass.

However, she does have her idiosyncrasies. While I drive, Jon tells me about the electric overdrive. It is controlled by a switch on the dashboard. It is used in high gear. A red light glows when the overdrive is switched on.

Jon tells me that you can use the overdrive at any speed above 40 mph. When Mabel's speed drops below 40 mph it must be switched off.

"AND," Jon says, "*Under no circumstances*, should you shift into reverse when the red light is on."

That would run the overdrive backwards and trash its innards and leave us dead in the water. It sounds a little complex, but it shouldn't be a problem. Jon will be here to slap me upside the head, if I slip up.

But the overdrive turns out to be a real joy. It makes flying down the interstate a very comfortable experience. Unlike other Classic sports cars built in Europe in the 1950s, Mabel is right at home on the interstate at any speed.

Most cars built in Europe back when Mabel was new had smaller, one and two liter engines. They had to work hard to cruise at 70 mph. This led Americans to think that most European cars were slow or unreliable because they weren't designed for Interstate travel.

But not Mabel. She just purrs along at 80 mph with loads to spare. As we eat up the miles traveling north up through the big San Joaquin valley, we easily stay with any traffic. She has plenty of power. This is really Grand Touring.

Many miles farther up the road we change drivers once again. Now "*Star Wars*" is pounding out of the speakers as we fly along the Interstate. I doze in the passenger's seat. As I close my eyes, my mind takes me away to a time long, long ago in a galaxy far, far away, and I boldly go where no man had gone before.

I am thinking of the coldness of deep space, but I am now feeling very warm. I open my eyes and notice the hot sun is beating down on us. It's getting hot in our open car. I start shedding clothes. Next, I slap on some suntan lotion. I smear on some lip grease and put on my sunglasses. I pull my baseball cap down tightly over my head. I make sure the bill shades my face. Now, I am ready.

"Sure is hot," I mumble.

"What?" Jon is paying attention to his driving.

"It's hot." I repeat.

"Yea, must be at least 85 degrees...maybe 90."

I disagree. "It's not that hot...it's not over 75."

"Eighty-five plus."

"Jon, I was raised in this valley and I know the temperature. Remember, it's a dry heat... and you come from the Seattle area... you don't know what dry heat is.

"No. It's hotter than 85."

"Seventy-five."

"Eighty-five plus." I hear him mutter. He's so stubborn.

Just then the radio newscaster breaks into our conversation with a report that several fires had been spotted in the high Sierras near Lake Tahoe. They are probably the result of the unusually dry summer and lightning strikes.

"See," I retort smugly, "this kind of dry heat is normal for this time of year."

As we continue north it seems to be that we are gaining altitude gradually. The road is straight and long. Jon and I don't talk much now. We just drive. Mabel's exhaust harmonizes with the music from the radio. The two sounds blend together and make new, mysterious, random harmonies. After a while it is difficult to separate the two.

A few hours later we see Redding in the distance.

"Redding coming up...we have to turn west onto Highway 299 and head toward Weaverville." That's Jon, always stating the obvious.

As I am driving again, I point out, "You may have to help me with the road signs."

Jon straightens up and adjusts his glasses, "Sure thing."

We enter Redding and I slow Mabel down to about 30 miles an hour.

"There it is...up ahead."

I turn west at the intersection. We drive through town and head toward the mountains. As we leave Redding we are back cruising at 60 miles an hour.

"The road to Weaverville goes up a pretty steep mountain pass," Jon tells me.

"That's Trinity Lake[2] coming up on our left," Jon adds just as I see blue water in the distance. The road runs like a gentle ribbon across the fingers of the lake and through forested hills toward the mountains.

As we start up the pass, I happen to look down at the gauges and notice Mabel's temperature is starting to get warmer than normal.

I point at the gauge. "Jon, is this normal?"

He looks. "Awww...sour owl poop."

"Is that good?" I question.

"No," Jon explains. "During the rebuild, I changed the stock, mechanical fan for an electric fan. I thought it would improve the cooling system and reduce the drag on the engine. It should have *improved* cooling. Now it looks like the fan I used wasn't big enough. Darn."

"What do you want me to do?" I am growing a little nervous.

---

[2] For more information visit www.trinitylakeresort.com/

"I'll watch the temperature. You watch the road!"

Sure, I'll watch the road. My eyes dart back and forth between the gauge and the road as we charge up the ever steepening hills. Mabel really grips the road, so I start taking each curve a little faster. I'm making a run for the summit. The gauge is inching higher and higher.

"Keep going, Ev, just keep going."

So I keep going. My stomach starts to tighten. Here we are hundreds of miles from home, not even over our first mountain pass and already the threat of engine failure looms large in my mind. Is this going to be a continuing problem? Will we be stuck in the mountains with a broken car and no one to call on? Will our trip end here? Is this the end of all our plans?

As we climb, I try to use as light a throttle as I can. Mabel has a lot of torque so I just 'float' up the hills and try not to lose too much speed on the corners. As we climb higher, so does the temperature gauge. Finally, just as we crest the summit, it peaks...still below the boiling point. I get off the throttle...down the hill we coast...down goes the temperature. Whew, we made it... I start to relax.

I turn to Jon, "... uhhh...about the trip through the Trinity Alps...ahhhh...is Mabel going to be okay?...huh?"

"Oh don't worry, Ev. It's a lot cooler higher up and the passes aren't as steep or as long." Jon's voice has the firmness of conviction.

We drive on, down a road that wanders through a green forest. Mabel is handling the curves really well. Before long, the temperature problem is forgotten and

I'm really enjoying the drive to Weaverville. This is really livin'.

We slow down as we pull into town. We see old dusty pickups and beat up cars sitting next to old wooden buildings. They look right at home. Once in a while a modern building comes into view but as we pass we notice it is only a front. The rest of the building looks like the other old wooden buildings.[3]

I see a couple of 4-wheel drive pickups with their lower parts covered with mud. Their metal sides are scratched and dented. These pickups are not like the 4-wheel drive trucks with their thousands of lights, shiny chromed wheels, massive knobby tires, and riding 18 feet off the ground that I see running around the Bay Area. The trucks in this town are real working trucks.

"Jon, I'm really hot and thirsty."

"Want to stop for a beer?"

"No."

"How about a soda?"

"No, I don't want a soda."

"Water?"

"No, I'm thirsty, not dirty."

"How about a nice, ice cold Root Beer Float in a frosty mug?" He says with a big wide grin.

There is an ear-splitting screech and smoke boils out of Mabel's tires as I slam on the brakes and slide to a stop in front of an ice cream store.

"How about here?" I offer mildly, turning to Jon.

---

[3] Visit www.weavervilleinfo.com/ for more information.

He's still crawling up out of the foot well and climbing back up into the passenger seat.

"What happened?" He looks around in shock.

"Ice cream store." I say pointing.

"Ice cream store? I thought we hit something."

"You said ice cold Root Beer Float in a frosty mug." I yell back.

A horn is honking behind us. I look back and see a line of cars. So what if we're blocking traffic. There are no parking spaces here anyway. But nice person that I am, I shift Mabel into gear, drive down the street and pull into a service station that has a canopy. We need the shade.

"I'll get the gas if you go get the floats."

"Deal." He's out of the car and down the street toward the ice cream store before I can say anything.

As I finish gassing Mabel up he is back with two large paper cups with frost on their sides, just dripping frothy goodness.

"How are these?" He teases.

"Got the spoons?"

"Right here, wrapped up in my shirt pocket." He's got a big smile.

I quickly pull Mabel over to a parking stall in the service station. Jon and I sit down under a shade tree. We slowly drink our cool refreshments. After the heat of the valley, they are just wonderful.

"How much fuel did we take?" Jon is just finishing his float.

"Twelve and a half gallons," I answer.

Jon pulls out his hand calculator and quickly punches the buttons.

"Nineteen point three miles per gallon." He replies proudly.

"That's not bad."

"Yeah, especially considering that we were driving at high speed and including the mountain pass and all."

"Well, you want to go over to Clark's?" After all, that's why we are here, to get together with our traveling buddy.

"Yes, we still have a long way to go today."

We climb into Mabel and I start her up. I just love the sound of those twin exhausts every time she starts. I always give the throttle a couple of extra pumps just to hear her roar. What a sound. We pull out of the station onto the side street where it enters Main Street. Traffic is thin...only one motorcycle coming down the road. It slows down, turns onto our street and as it drives by us the rider yells something at me.

"What'd he say?" I ask Jon.

"I don't know, . . .but he's coming back."

Probably some local drunk biker wanting to cause us some problem just because we're driving a foreign car. I look around the cockpit for a weapon. Nothing. Now I'm worried. There's too much cross traffic to gun it and get out of here.

The biker pulls up next to us. He yells, "Get that piece of trash off the street or we'll run you out of town."

Holy cow poops. We've got a fight brewing. I open the car door with one hand and fumble with the seat belt with the other. I want to be standing up if I get hit.

"Do you have a problem?" I ask as I pull myself up getting ready to fight (or flee depending what happens next).

The biker pulls up his visor and I'm looking at Clark's face.

"Clark," I yell. "You jerk...you had me so shook up, I was ready to rumble."

We laugh and shake hands. Jon joins us and we start having our reunion right there in the middle of the street. Clark is the first to realize where we are.

"Hey, we'd better get out of the street. Why don't you follow me back to my place?"

Jon and I climb back into Mabel and we follow Clark two miles out of town and down a dirt road to his house.

His house has shingle siding, parquet decking, black trim and sits under a big spreading shade tree with a little babbling brook to listen to when you go to the bathroom. So this is what it is like to live in the mountains. Maybe someday I'll get enough gumption to leave the city and become a mountain man too.

We finally get to rest, sit in the shade and talk a spell. Clark mentions that we must be hot because he'd heard on the news that it was over 95 degrees in the valley.

Jon looks over at me and flashes me a big grin.

I just hate it when he's right.

3 – Boiling Over

As we continue discussing our planned route, Clark mentions that it's a good thing we're not taking I-5 North of Redding. He's heard news about some big forest fires in that direction. Since our route takes us around the affected area, I don't pay much attention.

Finally, it is time to go. We stop at a store on the

edge of town and fill the cooler with ice, milk, and soft drinks. Jon admits he's glad I brought the cooler. I buy a few munchies and away we go, up Highway 3.

The sun is still blazing away, so I put on some more suntan lotion and lip grease. We look behind us and see Clark, 25 yards back, following us on Moonshadow, his Honda Gold Wing.

Knowing Moonshadow had a 2-way CB radio, we had temporarily installed a CB in Mabel before we left so we could communicate on the trip[4]. We immediately started to chatter with Clark. It was enjoyable to be able to talk without the usual yelling conversation. Like…

"Hey, Clark, look at that beautiful waterfall."

"What?"

Again you'd say "Waterfall" and point.

He'd yell back "No, I'm not thirsty."

Yes, the CB made all the difference in the world.

The valley leads north from Weaverville through much evidence of once busy mining. The rocks indicate that the valley has been moved around by miners busy searching for gold. This is another beautiful mountain area. Finally, we come to the end of the valley where the road forks to the left and we begin the climb over Scott Mountain pass.

The road turns out to be one of those little narrow, tight twisting roads that wind up the side of a forested mountain. There are many left and then right hairpin turns. Mabel takes them all in stride at first. Then…

As we climb higher, Mabel's temperature, once again starts to do likewise. I offer Jon a piece of ice to chew on. I take one also. It sure makes us feel better. Unfortunately, it doesn't do a thing for Mabel—and she's the one that needs it.

---

[4] Citizen Band Radios, or "CBs," allowed easy public 2-way communications. CB radios were popular before Cell phones were invented. https://en.wikipedia.org/wiki/Citizens_band_radio

Jon observes that this is a much steeper grade than he remembered from the last time he went over it. And worse, it's lot hotter. This isn't looking so good. The road stays tight and twisty. We cannot drive Mabel over 40 mph due to the twisty road, and at this slow speed, she's not getting enough cooling air through her radiator. Once again Mabel's temperature gauge is climbing. Pretty soon, it is over 90 centigrade.

Now it reads 95 C. (Water normally boils at 100C.)

A few miles farther it is up to 98 C.

I'm getting real nervous. This is no fun.

"Hey Jon, maybe we'd better pull over" I suggest quaveringly.

Jon keeps driving.

The temperature reaches the 100 degrees centigrade mark and then, the needle keeps edging up—clear off scale.

NOT GOOD! Nervously, I unbuckle my seat belt. I might need to jump. I expect the radiator is going to blow up at any moment. I can just see the hood bending over the windshield and our open cockpit filling with boiling water. And that would really cook us. It'd take the meat right off our bones.

I am not going to be here.

I look at the temperature gauge again. The needle is definitely past 100 C, and up against the pin separating the temperature gauge from the oil pressure gauge just above it. Mabel is now definitely overheated.

I say "Jon" and point at the needle as I lift myself out of the seat. I am leaving.

Jon's shoulders sag. He pulls over and turns the engine off (big mistake). The radiator promptly starts to boil over. Immediately, Jon restarts the engine and pulls the knob to open the hood. I am already out of the car. Quickly I run back, open the trunk and get the water jug. Then I run back to the front of the car, raise the hood, and pour water over the front of the hot radiator. This is an old trick I learned working in service stations as a teenager. Immediately, the temperature drops back down to well under the 90 C mark.

"Wow," Jon slaps his forehead and yells at me, "Quick, get in."

This is only a temporary fix so I jump back in the car and Jon, Mabel, and I begin our Life-and-Death run for the summit. We will be safe on the other side, IF we can make it.

From what I have heard, this part of the Trinity National Forest is extremely beautiful and a wonderful place to take a slow Sunday drive up the twisty mountain road.

Today our drive is entirely different. We accelerate up a short straight away, scream around a turn, charge up another straight away, brake for another turn, meanwhile, looking vainly for the top of the hill and slipping sidewise glances at the temperature gauge which is beginning to climb again. As we charge up the hill we watch as the needle climbs too. Higher and higher we go. Ever upwards moves the gauge. This is a race between us and Mabel's temperature gauge.

"It's a matter of being light on the gas in a high enough gear and try to not lose momentum on the corners so as to get the maximum speed with the smallest amount of engine heat." Jon shouts over the rushing wind.

"The road is so tight that speeds over forty-five are just not possible. At these slow speeds, Mabel isn't getting enough air through her radiator to cool off. It's all my fault." At least he is honest about it.

"How do you like it when I'm wrong, Ev?"

Actually, I don't.

I know the trees are flying by, but I don't inhale the fragrance of the pine forest or see the mountain tops against the cobalt blue sky. I feel the tightness in my stomach as I visualize us, lying dead in the sun, our dry, white bones spread eagled beside the wreckage of a 1955 rusting roadster named Mabel. I am not really enjoying our trip through the Trinity Alps.

Suddenly, we reach the summit of Scott Mountain Pass at 5617 feet and burst out of the forest, just as the water temperature edges past the 100C mark. To our relief, the temperature begins to fall as we start down the other side of the mountain. I look in the rear-view mirror and Clark is right behind us, about 25 yards back. Whew, our first day out and already, we've had serious trouble—twice.

We stop at the bottom of the pass at a stream called Scott Creek. We rest and refill the water jug. If we need to, we want to be able to spray water on the radiator again. That water jug is looking smaller all the time. Just in case, we also fill up some empty soft drink bottles. Meanwhile, Clark sits and watches us, looks at his watch, shakes his head, and yawns. Moonshadow is obviously keeping its cool better than Mabel.

About this time, Jon reports he's seeing sprinklers in the forest.

Evidently, someone was irrigating their property in the woods, using some type of revolving sprinkler. However, every time Jon can get Clark's or my attention, the sprinklers are out of sight. (I did see them one time, but did I tell Jon. Nooooooo way!)

We keep telling him the heat is affecting his eyesight.

"Take two aspirins and call us in the morning."

Clark and I are having fun teasing Jon. It helps relieve the tension of the past few hours.

We leave Scott Creek and turn East toward Highway 5 and Gazelle. This will be our short cut out of the Trinity Alps to I-5. Then we will back track about twenty miles to Weed where we will pick up highway 97 North. Jon wants to stop at a First Aid Station because he thinks the heat is making him hallucinate. I offer Jon another piece of ice. He takes it. I check the rear-view mirror. Yep, Clark is still there.

As we approach Gazelle we come out from behind a small hill and there, protruding above the barren landscape, is the giant, magnificent pyramid of Mount Shasta. What a sight. It is conical shaped, and it looks like the biggest snow-covered ant hill I have ever seen. The sight of it just overwhelms me.

I'm so excited; I forget the CB and yell at Clark, "Look at the size of that mountain."

Over the CB, I hear his reply, "No, I'm not thirsty."

At Weed, we stop for gas and water. Mabel gets a long, cool drink of refreshing water--four quarts long to be exact. She was really thirsty. We decide to let her cool off, and we all take a rest break. We have made it out of the tight twisty mountain passes and we are still in one piece.

Ahead lays well over a thousand miles of adventure.

4 – A VIP in Nowhere

It is afternoon before we take off on Highway 97 out of Weed. The road climbs up onto a high plateau. Up on the plateau the land is flat and barren. After a while we start to see timber. We are approaching the Oregon border. As we get closer, more trees appear and soon we are driving through pine forests.

While crossing the river at Klamath Falls, I'm impressed by something I've never seen before. Hundreds and hundreds of logs, laced together in giant rectangles, floating in the river. Wow. They are waiting to be pulled into the lumber mill and turned into everything from 12 x 12 timbers to toothpicks. I have only seen things like this in pictures.

Jon's not impressed. He's seen things like this lots of times. He says he will show me log flows that will blow this away. Ok, but nevertheless, I'm still impressed.

We leave Klamath Falls and continue on 97 past Upper Klamath lake[5], the small town of Chiloquin and out into another flat, forested area. Our fuel is ok, but Moonshadow, is getting a little low. Clark radios that he needs Super Unleaded which might be hard to find. A fine time to mention it. There aren't many Service stations out here. We start checking each station whenever we see one, but no "Super."

---

[5] Visit www.lakelubbers.com/upper-klamath-lake-1272/

At one point, Jon and I pull into a station and slide to a stop in the gravel with the CB antenna whipping back and forth over our heads. A teenage boy runs over to see what we want.

"Wow, nice car," he remarks.

"Thanks," I reply. "Have you got any Super Unleaded?"

"No," he says as he looks us over from front to back, "but you can get some in Chemult, about ten miles up the road." His eyes are getting wider and wider.

I pick up the CB mike, "Clark, gas in ten miles."

"Roger." comes back Clark's reply as he pulls Moonshadow into the station behind us.

"Thanks," I shoot back at the young man as both roadster and motorcycle speed off. I can't help looking in the mirror and see him still standing there, eyes bugging out and mouth wide open.

We must seem like real VIP's to him, in our hot little red roadster with a 2-way radio and motorcycle escort. Probably the wildest thing he's seen all month? . . . or maybe all year?

At Chemult[6] we decide to stop and feed Mabel and Moonshadow their fuel and get some food for us.

This service station is a family affair. The owner and his fourteen-year old daughter are pumping the gas...or at least the father is. The young girl is so excited over seeing Mabel; she's totally forgotten to pump the gas. She keeps running around asking questions and demanding to be taken for a ride. When Jon declines politely, she gets more excited and starts teasing him by snapping him on his rear with a towel. She alternates between running her hands over Mabel's fenders, hood, and sides, and snapping Jon with the towel. This is one time I'm happy to *not* be Mabel's owner.

Jon is taking it all good naturedly, but I could see that her father has a dim view of it. While he finishes topping off Moonshadow's tank he mumbles to Clark that he is at

---

[6] Visit http://chemult.org/ for information about Crater Lake.

his wits end as to what to do with her. Oh, the pleasures of fatherhood.

After we pay for the gas, we stop at the main cafe in town for supper. The waitress is very friendly and chats with us while we eat. Jon has veal cutlets with mashed potatoes and a tossed salad. I think the Williamsburg Creole Chicken sounds good. When it comes, I discover I am right, it is the best I've ever had. Clark has a Chile burger with extra onions. He then orders a bottle of soy sauce and squirts that on top. Jon and I just look at each other. I'm beginning to wonder if Clark has lived in the Mountains too long.

During dinner Jon gets up a few times to go check on Mabel. Everyone entering and leaving the cafe has been stopping and looking Mabel over. Some people can't resist. They reach out a hand and run it over Mabel's beautiful maroon finish. They don't know that a little dust is like fine sandpaper under their hand and could easily mar the finish. However, most onlookers are respectful of the effort that has obviously gone into Mabel's restoration and refrain from touching her. I can see Jon appreciates that.

While we're paying our bill, a man at the counter strikes up a conversation with Jon when he realizes he is the owner of the Jag outside. He claims to be very knowledgeable about Jaguars, but he has some rather uncomplimentary opinions. He says he was a one-time Austin Healy owner. I guess some British car owners have negative opinions about other British cars. Probably they are also pretty competitive, much like the rivalry between Ford and Chevy in America. It is too bad he doesn't own that Austin Healy now. It would be fun to go out and dust him off in a high-speed run. Mabel has long legs that no normal Austin Healy could hope to keep up with.

After our stop in Chemult, we are on the road again and heading for Bend, Oregon. Mabel is running strong and she seems very happy with all the attention she's getting every time we stop. We are discovering she attracts a crowd wherever we go. I see it makes Jon proud and I'm happy to be a part of it.

As the sun sets, the forests disappear against the night sky, replaced by headlights cutting through the darkness. I check the rear-view mirror, and, yep, the single head light of Clark riding Moonshadow is there, following us. Why is he always behind us? Why not in front? Maybe he doesn't trust our brakes? Maybe our driving? Maybe us? I chuckle at the thought.

We roll into Bend[7] and look for a good place to stay. We are tired after the first long day on the road. We've come almost six hundred miles from the bay area in California, a long way.

Ahh, the Cimarron Motel. They charge the three of us thirty-eight bucks for a room. Clark had been planning to find a park and sleep under a tree. We convince him (with very little effort) that a nice warm shower in the morning would feel better than being rained on ...or attacked by a dog.

Mabel is very dirty. She has a lot of miles of road dirt on her and about two million bugs on her face. So,

---

[7] Visit www.el.com/to/bend/

before we go to bed, Jon takes her down to the friendly Do-It-Yourself car wash and gives her a shower. With all the attention she is getting we want her to look clean and spiffy for the next day's run. Not good to have the star of the show with bugs in her teeth.

It *has* been a long day. And it has been an *exciting* day. However, everything is going smoothly now. Sure, poor Mabel got all lathered up a couple of times earlier in the day but, after all, those mountain passes had been steep, the day had been very hot, and Jon admitted to causing it by changing the stock fan for an electric one.

But, when she's not climbing up slow mountain passes, Mabel has been running cool and we've had no more temperature trouble once we'd crossed over the border into Oregon.

We decide to go to one of the local watering holes and visit. We stay there quite a while, going over the day's exciting events and catching up on personal events. Finally, exhausted, I returned to the motel and went to bed.

Jon and Clark partied on late into the night.

5 – Smoke… And Ghosts

Sunday morning, the second day of our trip, greets us with the sounds of car doors opening and closing... trunks on cars being slammed shut...men and women talking in loud voices...children's laughter and giggling.

"What's all the noise?" Jon mumbles.

"It'd have been quieter in the park," Clark mutters.

"I think all the noise is coming from in here." is my contribution.

I get hit with a pillow, Clark's boot and one smelly sock.

"Hey, knock it off!"

Clark's other boot misses me and hits the wall with a loud thump. Someone pounds on the wall and we hear a muffled voice... "Hey, knock it off in there!"

We look at each other. "I guess it's time to get up."

Everyone showers and tries to wake up. We're all happy because we are on vacation. We finally finish dressing and packing Mabel and Moonshadow.

"Where are we eating?" I ask.

"Let's drive down the road and find a nice place." suggests Clark.

I'm driving Mabel as we leave the motel and head North through town. About ten blocks away Jon pats my leg and points, "How about that Denny's over there?""Sure, sounds good to me." I turn around and get Clark's attention. I point to the Denny's in the distance.

He holds up his left hand, making a circle with his index finger and thumb.

"Clark says okay." I grin and punch Jon in the side.

"Ooofff!" "What'd you do that for?"

"You touched my leg back there."

"So?"

"I don't like to be touched by men."

He looks at me, grins mischievously and then immediately throws his arms around my neck.

"Awww, Evvie, how about a little huggie poo?"

"Stop it!" I yell, while Mabel swerves from lane to lane. Jon falls back into his seat, laughing wildly.

I get Mabel under control again and we approach Denny's. I signal a left turn, roar around the corner and pull up to the curb.

Clark pulls up next to us, "Now girls, no fighting in the car."

I glare at him.

Jon gets out, runs around the car, grabs my door and swings it open, "May I help you out...madam." He bows and sweeps his arm under him in a very humble gesture.

"I'll get it myself." I grumble as I step out.

Jon and Clark are breaking up, laughing.

"You guys ready for breakfast?"

"Yep, we're ready," Jon answers.

We enter Denny's and ask for a window seat so we can keep an eye on the vehicles. We are ushered to a large table. Jon and I order the standard breakfast. Clark asks for a bowl of dry corn flakes and a beer. When it comes, he pours the beer over the corn flakes, adds a little sugar and digs in.

He looks up and sees Jon and I frozen in place, staring.

"Good for a hangover," he says and continues eating. Whew, I hope I never have a hangover like he has.

While we eat, we enjoy a show. People are looking at Mabel and Moonshadow. First a mob gathers around Mabel and then another mob gathers around the Honda. Jon and Clark smile a lot.

We finish our breakfast, pay the bill and go outside. The sun is getting higher in the sky. We stretch and walk over to Mabel and the bike. We take our time getting ready. With full stomachs and stiff legs, it is a little difficult finding room to fit everything.

I start Mabel, and we head north out of town. Hey, the forests are gone. During the night we have moved back onto a flat, open plain. It's strange how the land changes like that when you don't even notice it.

Yesterday we were high in the mountains, last night we were deep in the forest, and today we find ourselves on a high plateau-like prairie which resembles the open plains of Nebraska.

As I'm driving, the highway stretches ahead of me like a dark colored ribbon leading us to the far horizon. On either side of the road are vast open sections of wheat fields. The wheat isn't tall yet, just young eager stalks pushing their heads up to the morning sun. This gives the land a "crew cut" appearance; it is totally unlike the flat brown land in the San Joaquin Valley that we'd seen only yesterday morning. Was that only yesterday? It seems like ages ago.

Here and there, small white farm houses and red barns dot the golden prairie land. In the distance a dusty cloud rises into the sky. As we get closer, we can see a farmer on an old tractor pulling some type of implement that churns up the earth. A dryness fills my mouth. The water isn't handy, so I decide to let it be dry. That farmer's mouth must be a lot dryer than mine. I squeeze the throttle a little more and we speed off down the dark ribbon of highway.

It feels like this land goes on forever.

We crest a small hill and see a town far up ahead, one of those semi-small collections of buildings that spring up whenever railroad tracks and roads meet in the Midwest.

"Madras," Jon says in my right ear. "Looks like a good place to stop for gas."

I look at the gas gauge and agree.

"Call Clark," I reply.

We mellow into town--a silver motorcycle trailing a red roadster, both dry. We want water and Mabel wants a gas pump to drink from.

We notice that the town looks strangely quiet. Not much going on at this time of the morning. We wonder what it was that made people pick this little spot on the plains to start a town. It certainly is clean and tidy looking town, but not very busy.

At the far end of town, we find a service station and pull in to clean windshields and fill gas tanks.

"According to the map, this is the biggest town in these parts," Clark reports, sliding his map back into his jacket as we make plans to leave.

"I guess" I reply, "but it's kinda hard telling where these "parts" begin and end, out here on the prairie."

He chuckles at that and we pull our vehicles back onto the highway and are once again out on the open plains.

Jon pipes up. "Ev, there is a ghost town up ahead I'd like to see. I don't know exactly how far it is so keep your eyes open."

"I visited there years ago," he continues, "My grandfather actually worked around there as a young man driving a horse drawn freighter." Jon pulls a road map out of a side pocket...unfolds it... and immediately starts chasing it around the windy cockpit. Finally he subdues it...looks at it closely and, as we zoom pass a turnoff, yells, "Turn there!"

I quickly step on the brakes, looking for a place to turn off. Finally, I see a place where I can make it. I stop, shift into what I think is low gear and let out the clutch. We shoot backwards. Oops, I'm in reverse. I stop again. I find low, start again and make my U-turn back down the road to the exit we just passed.

But I sense something is wrong.

I look down on the dash and see a red light glowing. Oh No! In the excitement of missing the turn, I've done what Jon had warned me against. I've shifted into reverse with the overdrive on.

I turn off the switch. I tell Jon what I have done.

"Uh, Jon, I think I did a boo-boo." He goes white. The smell of something awful—something burning—is now engulfing the cockpit. Oh dear. This is not good.

I make the turnoff onto OR-293. I drive slowly, trying all the gears. Finally, I try the overdrive. It's still working. We both breathe a sigh of relief. Whew, that was close. Apparently, there was no permanent damage, except to our nerves—and our noses.

When we turn our attention back to where we are, we discover that we are traveling along Oregon highway 293. It appears to be a typical back country road. Rocks are scattered in fields on both sides, and cliffs loom in the distance. When we reach the top of the cliff, we enter the little town named Antelope.[8]

Just a few years ago, in 1984, this town had been the headquarters of guru Bhagwan Shree Rajneesh, and his group of followers. Since there were only a few people living there at the time, the Bhagwan's followers took over the town and voted to change its name to Rajneesh. Later after the sect's secretary stole the group's money, the Bhagwan was charged with immigration violation and returned to India. The townspeople voted to return the name to Antelope in 1985.

The old town looks deserted. An old garage with a pair of fifty-year-old gas pumps sits forlornly in the afternoon sun. We walk over to a two-story building with an old weathered sign reading IOOF. We look through dirty windows and see several mattresses strewn about on the old wood planked floor. We speculate that it had been a holding area for followers of the guru.

---

[8] Visit https://en.wikipedia.org/wiki/Antelope,_Oregon

There is no one on the streets. We drive up and down the main (and practically only) street. We feel as if people are looking at us from behind closed curtains. It gives us an eerie feeling. We turn onto OR-218, drive north out of town and leave this strange place behind us.

We are now heading for Shaniko, Oregon.[9] The road to Shaniko meanders through barren rolling hills, populated with a few small thirsty looking trees. As we approach the town, the road bends sharply to the left, down into a small gully and up the other side. To the east, the gully turns into a deep ravine. The pioneers who built the road could have kept going straight but that would have meant building a bridge. Build bridges? Not if they could help it. In Shaniko, we are back on US-97.

---

9 For more information visit

https://en.wikipedia.org/wiki/Shaniko,_Oregon

Shaniko is a true rarity. It is a *living* ghost town. Only about two dozen people live there, mainly involved in preserving what had once been a bustling town.

Shaniko was homesteaded by a German immigrant by the name of August Scherneckau in the 1800's. But because of the difficulty in pronouncing his name, it evolved into Shaniko (I had trouble even pronouncing Shaniko, until I heard it a few times).

Shaniko sits on a high desert plateau. In 1870, the first building, a saloon, was built north of the original homestead, and in 1900, the post office was built. On May of that year, the first train arrived, and a boom began that made Shaniko one of the wildest, woolliest towns of the early West—quite literally because Shaniko's principal product was wool.

The town expanded to six full blocks of hotels, saloons, gambling houses, livery stables, bawdy houses, and law offices. In one year, the train carried around 29,000 passengers. By 1902, Shaniko had become the "Wool Capital of the World," shipping 5 million pounds of wool.

Shaniko started to die when railroads were built farther south. In 1910 the railroads reached Madras and the next year they reached Bend. Shaniko began a very slow death. In 1934 the banks closed. In 1943 the train stopped running and Shaniko faded into history.

Arriving in town we can see motor vehicles from the past, slowly rusting away in open fields. Behind wooden sidewalks are old wood buildings with false fronts. Wagons, buggies, and even a stage coach sit gathering dust.

Never again will running horses pull them down dirt roads, carrying passengers to far off places. We drive through the town and turn around.

We find a parking place in front of an old building with a sign that reads "Saloon." Where else? We get out and walk slowly around town. As we step onto the sidewalks, dust puffs out from beneath our shoes. We look through dusty windows and see sunlight streaming through open holes in long neglected roofs. We check out many nooks and crannies. But in our search for treasures, someone has been there before us. All that is left is an old outhouse beside the road. "How quaint." I think. Later, I discover it was not just there to look at. That was really the place you went, when you had to go.

I go back to Mabel where I left my hat and put it on. The sun is really getting hot again. I sit down on a bench in front of the saloon.

A family playing tourist starts a conversation with me about how wonderful it must be to ride in a car like

Mabel. I immediately start to tell them how windy it is, how dirty you get with no windows to roll up, and how uncomfortable the seats are and on and on. After a few minutes they realize I am joking. They really enjoy my wild story.

I'm driving as we leave town. It's sad to be leaving. I want to spend more time here and pick up some more history from the locals--the type of history that's not written--the real dirt.

The real Shaniko is what I want to know about. But Shaniko "Oregon's Most Interesting Ghost Town," is still there, waiting, watching, ready for other travelers to stop, look and then move on.

A few miles down the road I spot the tourists from Shaniko parked beside the road. I step on the throttle and hit the horn. They recognize Mabel. Then they give us a wave.

We fly past them, crest a hill and they are gone, only a memory, just like Shaniko.

6 – A Brush with Death

We drive several miles in silence. We're just staring ahead as the road rolls under us. Finally, we arrive, hot and thirsty, at a little town called Grass Valley[10].

"You want something ice cold that'll take the road dust out of our parched mouths?" I ask.

"Yes, absolutely!" is Jon's reply.

We drive slowly through town looking left and right. Most of the buildings look deserted. On the right side of the street is a row of structures with boarded up windows and bleached, wooden sides. The afternoon sun is low in the west and shadows are creeping slowly up their faces, softening their harshness. We park there and walk across the street to a general store that is open.

I head straight to the cooler in the rear of the store and look at all the tempting refreshments. In the milk section I see a pint of "Strawberry Milk". That seems like a good idea. Jon and Clark have chilled cans of sodas in their hands as we walk to the counter.

"What'd you get?" Clark asks.

"Strawberry Milk," I answer.

"Strawberry Milk?" Jon's jaw drops.

"Yes," I reply, holding the carton up in front of them.

"Ukkkaaa." Clark frowns.

Jon shakes his head sadly.

---

[10] Visit https://en.wikipedia.org/wiki/Grass_Valley,_Oregon

We return to the cool shade and sit down. I open my carton and take a careful drink. I feel fresh strawberries washing across my taste buds. The cool liquid refreshes my mouth. Impressive.

I turn the carton around to read the label, expecting the ingredients to say: "Fresh Whole Milk mixed with plump ripe strawberries picked fresh from a garden tended by a sweet little old lady that washed each strawberry in fresh spring water before hand carrying them to the dairy next door."

I am astonished at the list of crap that is in that Strawberry Milk. Oh, the miracles of chemistry.

I take another drink. It still tastes like a fresh strawberry milkshake, a little thin, but a good strawberry taste. I am amazed. It is delicious.

As we finish, Clark stands up and stares down the street.

"That's an antique store over there and I think it's open."

I look and sure enough it is an antique store. I jump up and throw the empty carton into a trash barrel, "Let's go."

Clark and I walk quickly toward the store. I look back and Jon is still sitting in the shade.

"You coming with us?"

"No, I think I'll stay here and rest."

"Okay." I turn and follow Clark.

We go inside and discover; it's a real antique store. It is loaded with everything you can imagine. Primarily, there are things from old ranches and farms. A lot of them are heavy, forged implements that have taken a pounding in running a ranch. They are not broken but have been used hard. It's amazing they have managed to survive.

"Ev, come here, you'll love this," Clark calls out from the back of the store.

I walk down the crowded aisles and find Clark standing in front of an old cream separator.

It is made of stainless steel, about a foot in diameter and four feet tall with a handle coming out of the top. It looks like it could handle five gallons of milk at a time. I start to dream of the terrific dishes and desserts I could create with the cream from this beautiful, rare implement.

"How do you like this baby?"

"It is beautiful." I utter.

"Seventy-five bucks." Clark turned to me and smiled.

"I've got to have it."

"How you gonna carry it?"

I'm stunned into silence. Yes, how am I going to carry it home?

"You think it's too large for Mabel's trunk?"

Clark laughs.

"I'll be right back." I run toward the front of the store.

The man at the counter looks shocked as I slide to a stop in front of him.

"You got a U-Haul trailer rental in town?" I ask.

He starts laughing and then gets into a coughing fit. He is laughing, coughing, and pointing a finger at me. He's lost it.

I run back to Clark.

"Maybe I can send Jon home on the bus and I could put it in the passenger seat?" I'm excited.

Clark starts laughing again.

"You think it'll fit on the back of your Honda?"

Tears stream down Clark's face. He slumps to floor, holding his stomach, laughing uncontrollably.

I run down the aisle and past the counter. The man sees me and starts pointing, laughing and then starts coughing again.

This is serious. People are losing control around me. I need help and fast. I want that separator!

I run outside, down the street, waving my hands and yelling to Jon. Jon hears me, stands up and runs over to meet me.

"What happened? Is Clark hurt?"

"No, Clark's not hurt but I found a cream separator that I really, really need. I think it will fit nicely behind the passenger's seat. Excitedly, I explain my plan to Jon.

"What do you think, Jon? We can take it with us, right?"

Jon was straight to the point.

"No."

Sadly, I left my treasure in Grass Valley.

The road out of Grass Valley is downhill into a gulch--a very large gulch. At the bottom of the gulch is the Columbia River. I am looking forward to crossing the Columbia River.

The Columbia River was formed when the glaciers from the Ice Age melted. All that icy cold water found its way to the Pacific Ocean. I guess at the time, the river was miles wide and hundreds of feet deep. After the Ice Age there was a lot of ice, you know. It ripped everything out by the roots and carried it away. It left the land deeply scarred and devastated.

Over the years, I thought that vegetation would have grown back. I visualized timber covered cliffs overlooking a deep gorge with the mighty Columbia ripping deeper gouges in the river bottom, much like the Grand Canyon.

I anticipated stopping and listening to the mighty roar of the white water. I expected to see brave and adventurous men and women bouncing along on inflated crafts as they crashed into mountains of water and being blasted out the other side as they were being carried downstream by the mighty Columbia.

I could hardly wait.

It turns out the Columbia River, is a flat, wide, placid looking, slow moving *immense* waterway with barren

bluffs on either side. It looks like it never fully recovered from the time when the glaciers melted and sent those raging torrents of water cascading down the mountain sides. This is not the picture that I had in mind. I'm so disappointed. It is not like what I imagined. I want to leave right away. So we press on[11].

We cross the Columbia and enter Washington State. We're climbing up into some timber country again. We are between the cities of Goldendale and Toppenish, starting up a long, steep hill toward Satus Pass.

The traffic slows and then starts to back up. A motor home is slowly struggling up the steep grade a few vehicles ahead. Right in front of us, an old green Oldsmobile is leaving trails of white smoke. It is drifting into the cockpit. Jon and I are coughing and rubbing our eyes. The sun is beating down on us. With the heat, smoke and slow traffic, I am becoming upset.

"Rats!"

"This is like commuter traffic," Jon offers.

"Yes, a real mess," I respond. "What's it doing way out here?"

After a few miles of crawling along, we need fresh air and a breeze to cool off from the heat. The oncoming traffic is endless. I'm getting impatient (If only there was an opening in the traffic). Just then I hear a roar and see a huge cloud of white smoke bellowing from the Olds' exhaust as it shoots out into the left-hand lane that is now temporarily void of traffic. At last. My chance.

I stomp the gas pedal, and Mabel's jungle cat-like tendencies come alive. A deep growl erupts from her

---

[11] Contrary to Everett's opinion, The Columbia River Gorge is actually quite beautiful. For more information, see www.gonorthwest.com/Oregon/columbia/Columbia_River.htm

exhaust and we leap forward in pursuit of the smoking Olds—not unlike a hungry predator chasing after a scared, fleeing quarry.

We quickly catch up to the speeding car and now we're following closely behind its rear bumper as we fly past the line of traffic behind the motor home.

This is exciting. I'm feeling real good with the wind blowing away the heat and fresh air clearing our lungs. It feels wonderful. Just what we needed.

But then, my enjoyment turns to terror as the Olds dives into a small hole in the line of traffic, just in front of the motor home and leaves me in the left lane with nowhere to go. Worse, I see an oncoming car ahead, a car which has just appeared over a rise and is rushing toward us.

I am blocked, and in the left lane. (Gulp!)

I gently tap the brakes (locked those suckers up!) and I turn the wheel slightly to the right, (Spun it as hard as I could!), my intention being to slow down and fall in behind the motor home. But my action causes us to skid wildly and now, Jon and I find ourselves going sideways at sixty miles an hour amidst the sound of squealing tires and the smoke of burning rubber. We watch the motor home's side passing in front of Mabel's hood. (A few scenes from my life were also passing before my eyes.)

Jon screams "Oh God!" (I didn't even know he was religious.)

"EAAGH!" I scream back.

I let up on the brakes, flick the wheel back to the left and Mabel quickly dives for safety behind the motor home just as the speeding import (a tiny Citroen 2CV, no less) screams by, horn blaring; the driver shaking his fist. (He didn't have to honk, I saw him.)

I start breathing again. Wow. That was close. I look over at my good buddy Jon and see his fingers imbedded on the grab bar on the dashboard. His eyes are staring straight ahead. His body is frozen stiff. He's still waiting for the crash.

"Close, huh?" I offer.

He slowly turns and looks at me, his mouth opens, his lips move, no sound comes out.

"Cat got your tongue?" I continue.

Jon extracts his hands from the grab bar, curling his fingers as if he's going to choke someone. His facial expression is something to behold.

The CB interrupts "Hey, Ev, can you do that again. That looks like fun."

Jon turns, picks up the CB mike with curled fingers, glares coldly at Clark, opens his mouth and moves his lips. No sound comes out.

"No, I'm not thirsty," comes the reply from Clark.

We drive on, trying to calm down. We talk about how close we came to crashing and dying. I try to explain to Jon how I had gotten myself in that position - even trying to blame Mabel - saying "her brakes locked up." But, in the end, I admitted I had made a serious mistake that almost cost us our lives. Mabel was actually the one who saved us. After that, I drive more carefully.

We stop at Toppenish for fuel and food. Jon mentions that Toppenish has a large native Indian population (we have just passed through the Yakima

Indian reservation). We stop at an A&W and sure enough, all the help are Indians.

Jon and I both get a cheeseburger and a big glass of frosty root beer. Clark talks to the girl taking the order.

"I'll have a GU-GE, a DI-GU-NU-I and a GV-NO-TLE-NU" to drink

The girl giggles, smiles and says "Okay."

I looked at Clark and ask, "What did you order?"

Clark responds, "I really don't know, but an old girl friend told me if I was ever in the A & W in Toppenish, I should order it."

"Oh."

As Jon and I work on our cheeseburgers and enjoy that great root beer, we watch Clark struggle with his Raw Artichoke, Lye Dumplings in hot grease, and a Hominy Corn Drink.

I couldn't resist. "How is it?"

Clark smiles through clenched teeth, "Hey, this isn't bad. It's actually pretty good. You guys wanna try it?"

I feel my stomach jump and I know I am through eating. I excuse myself, put my unfinished cheeseburger down on the plate and get up. As I left, I look back. Jon is sneaking out the other exit, holding his hand over his mouth. We meet coming out of the men's room.

"If he does that to us again, I'm going to put sugar in his gas tank."

Jon looks very serious. "I'll help."

7 – A Bad Bump in a Bad Land

[NOTE: Interesting places along the way are: Goldendale,[12] Toppenish[13], and Yakima[14]]

We get back on Hwy 97 again and head for Wenatchee. We are hardly out of Toppenish when I ask…

"Say, where are we going to stay tonight?"

"Well...my brother has this big house in Wenatchee and I was thinking of crashing there."

"Did you call and let him know we were on the way?"

"Naw, I want to surprise him." Jon is grinning, is he kidding?

"Any motels in Wenatchee?"

"Motel? We don't need no stinking motels. My brother's place will be just fine." He looks serious…

"A big soft bed and three pillows is what I need."

"The floor will be fine." (Who's he trying to kid?)

I stare off into the distance. I am getting a motel.

"Have you noticed the volcanoes all around us?" Jon interrupts my pouting.

"Where?"

"There, in the distance." Jon's pointing ahead.

---

[12] Visit https://ci.goldendale.wa.us/

[13] Visit http://cityoftoppenish.us/

[14] Visit www.visityakima.com/

Squinting hard, I see a cone-shaped mountain in the far distance.

"And there's another one. Over there." Jon is indicating off to the west.

I see another cone-shaped mountain, larger than the last.

"Everett, we are traveling on a line between the Pacific and the North American Plate. Since these two plates are moving in different directions, they continually collide. This is what formed the Cascades Mountain's chain of volcanoes. These volcanoes let out some of the pressure from the plates' collisions. It has taken millions of years to create this geography."

The land off to the East is flat. Farms stretch out for miles. I feel like I can see the prehistorical time when this land was being attacked by exploding mountains. I listen and watch... waiting... waiting... "Are they going to blow their tops now?" I wait...and wait. Nothing.

"Jon, I can imagine it. Long ago, when these volcanoes were being formed, before life began, the heat must have been tremendous. Mountains of molten rock were pushed up through the Earth's crust, throwing huge clouds of gray ash into the sky, and rivers of red-hot steaming molten lava flowing down the mountain side."

I can feel Jon's eyes on me.

"And now they're still. They're silent, Jon. They're dead. Never again will they change the face of the earth or darken the skies."

I turn. Jon is looking at me.

"Ev, that is Mount St. Helens right there." He's pointing again. "You *do* remember Mount St. Helens, don't you?"

Oh yes, I remember.

In the spring of 1980, Mount St. Helens[15] erupted, underscoring the Cascades' volcanic origins. It started with a series of small earthquakes. Then, on May 18th came a tremendous explosion. The eruption flattened 250 square miles of forest. Clouds of ash and pulverized rock shot into the sky, some falling over 900 miles away. Rockslides avalanched down the steep slopes into Spirit Lake raising the water level 190 feet. Spirit Lake overflowed, mixing with the melting glaciers and ash from the burning forest. Newly formed brown and gray rivers flooded East and West down into the populated valleys destroying bridges, roads, crops, and homes killing 57 people in the process, including a real-life character named Harry Truman who elected to stay on his beloved Spirit Lake.

Mountain climbers, miles away, felt electricity arc off their ice axes by the energy that was released.

Oh Yes, I remember Mount St. Helens.

And there it is, right there, sitting silent, watching us.

We drive on through Yakima and head towards Ellensburg.

On the approach to Ellensburg, the highway starts down a long hill. At the speed we are traveling, the road starts to feel like a giant vibrator.

---

[15] To learn more about the stupendous eruption visit https://en.wikipedia.org/wiki/1980_eruption_of_Mount_St._Helens

"This road is really bumpy." I'm holding onto the grab bar.

Jon looks around at the road and then looks back.

"It's getting worse. I'm having trouble steering."

"May-be we bet-ter slo-w d-do-wn." I offer through chattering teeth.

Jon slows down but, as he does, the rear of the car really starts jumping up and down. "Wham," "Wham," "Wham," comes from under Mabel; she is literally bouncing down the road.

Jon pulls over and stops. Clark pulls up alongside and looks down at us.

"Hey, Mabel keeps throwing her butt up in the air." Jon and I both stare coldly at Clark.

"Yes, we noticed."

We get out and inspect the rear of the car. At first nothing seems out of place. Then, we discover that the right rear tire has a large bulge, right in the middle of the tread. We've been driving on a tire with a big, cantaloupe sized wart on it—a very hard one at that. It looks ugly, like some kind of cancer.

We dump our luggage out on the ground in a pile to get at the spare and Jon's jack. After pulling off the tire, we examine the damage. It looks like the inside belt has separated and is pushing the tread outward making the bulge. We scratch our heads. This is very strange especially considering the tire doesn't have five thousand miles on it. Of course it had to happen at a time like this, out in the middle of nowhere.

Now I happen to notice how far away from civilization we really are. Around us, the land seems to go on forever in all directions. Here we are stuck on the side of the road with our luggage piled out on the ground and our car jacked up. What few cars we see, blow right on past us. A bad tire may sound trivial, but way out here, it takes on a whole new perspective. I'm thankful we thought to check the spare before the trip.

Soon our luggage is back in the trunk and we are on our way again. Replacing the tire fixed our rough ride, although now we don't have a spare. But Clark quotes some statistics on the astronomical possibility of having two flat tires on the same trip. His logic sounds reasonable to Jon and me. So we plan on just making the rest of the trip on the spare. If absolutely necessary, we could put the damaged tire back on and limpity bump a short distance into a service station.

Jon is still somewhat worried as we make our way into Wenatchee, "The Apple Capital of the World." We talk about the tire. Suppose we have another flat? Should we buy another tire? Should we gamble? Worry, worry, worry. It really drains me. I'm wondering if that wild slide we took back at Satus Pass, heated the tires and caused some internal damage? Naw, that couldn't be it. Could it?

I'm really looking forward to getting to Wenatchee. Supposedly, it has lots of blue sky and sunshine. It is North Central Washington's hub and offers attractive accommodations.[16]   In April, the Washington State's Apple Blossom Festival is hosted there. I have also heard about the nationally acclaimed Ohme Gardens.

---

[16] Visit www.gonorthwest.com/Washington/cascades/Wenatchee/Wenatchee.htm

Over a period of 50 years, a family developed this immaculate alpine wonderland out of an arid wasteland. They started this garden on a dry sagebrush bluff and by the careful use of water and a lot of hard work, created a lush green garden where small animals run freely and wildflowers grow in abundance. It is listed as one of the leading gardens in America.

However, by the time we arrive in Wenatchee, everyone is exhausted. Jon is over heated, discouraged and more than a little grumpy. Clark and I try to talk to him, but he doesn't cheer up. I am tired, and hot too. Here we are, the second day on the road, and so far Mabel's gotten lathered up twice and thrown a shoe. Not to mention our brush with death. Already we'd had more adventure than we'd expected.

We stop at a service station for gas, and Jon uses the phone to call his brother. But he's not home. Just our luck. Jon's plan is not working. Then Clark suggests we find a motel with a swimming pool and go soak our bodies. Everyone quickly agrees. We'll just find his brother later.

A drive down the main street offers us many choices. One in particular, the Holiday Lodge, catches our attention. It has a pool, hot tub, and a sauna. Within a short time we are all up to our necks in the pool's cool, refreshing water. We linger a long time. After that we soak in the hot tub. By the time we climb out, we are really hungry, so we check in at the main desk for a place to eat. We are directed to the Four Seasons Restaurant in East Wenatchee[17].

Traveling through town, we turn left and drive over a bridge. We make a right turn at the end of the bridge and just to the right, we see the restaurant. Upon entering we request a window seat.

We are led to a room with large glass windows overlooking a spectacular view of Wenatchee and the twin bridges spanning the Columbia River. Below, in the slow-moving Columbia, jet skiers are leaving rooster tails far behind them as they zoom back and forth. The sun is setting behind Wenatchee's skyline. It is bathing everything in the warm glow. What a beautiful sight this is.

We order a tray of drinks. As we talk and drink; we become cheerful, even funny. We are having a good time again. We finally decide to have dinner, and being in Washington, I order grilled salmon.

I am served a perfectly grilled salmon filet and zucchini slices sautéed in butter and sherry. Next to them are carrots, sliced like thin wood shavings, quick boiled, and curled beside the salmon. Italian parsley decorated the top. Scrumptious.

Jon is having a medium rare Prime Rib with baked potato, and a mixture of steamed vegetables. That also looks delicious.

Clark claims he is going to have one of his home town favorites. Frankfurters, stuffed with sauerkraut,

---

[17] Today the author could not find a reference to the Four Seasons Restaurant.

served over a bed of cold rice sautéed in goose fat. He wants a lukewarm coke to wash it down. Jon and I look at each other. We wonder what is it with our friend's choices of food? When our dishes come, we both eat slowly, letting the fine flavors enhance our good feelings. I don't know what Clarks food was doing to him.

After the table is cleared, the waiter asked if we would like dessert. I order Strawberry Meringues Chantilly. The Meringue shells had been baked on a cookie sheet and cooled. A mixture of clean strawberries, powdered sugar, and a touch of brandy fill the shells. A liberal amount of whipped cream is spooned on top. A fresh strawberry, with leaves, is placed on top the whipped cream. Jon chooses a small bowl of spumoni ice cream.

Clark reached in his pocket and pulled out a Snickers candy bar.

After dinner we order liqueurs and sip slowly. With the mellow drinks and warm conversation, we melt into our chairs. We stay a long time. With great effort, Jon rises out of his chair, goes to the far side of the room, and takes a picture of Clark and I with sun the going down over the Columbia River in the background.

We leave the Four Seasons fat, and happy.

Back at the motel Jon calls his brother again, and this time he's home. Clark and I both decline the offer to join him and he leaves to visit his brother.

It is *Ruthless People* on TV and we *do* have our priorities.

8 – We Reach the Frontier

Monday is only the third day of our trip. It comes too early. I feel that I could sleep a few more hours. However, we rise and check out the vehicles and, uh oh, someone had opened a door against Mabel's right side and left what looked like a really large scrape. It turned out to be just paint from the car whose door had hit Mabel. A little rubbing compound removed all traces, except for a very small dent that you could hardly see. Jon said that when he first saw it, he felt like the whole side was caved in. Not a good way to start a day.

We check with the lady at the front desk for a good breakfast place. She recommends the Red Rooster. When we arrive, Jon parks Mabel sideways, taking up two parking spaces. I tell him you can't do that. But as I am flapping my gums, Clark pulls up and parks next to us. Two vehicles, two parking places, what the heck, why not? After the motel incident, Jon wants to protect the car. I guess it's not a bad idea. We go in and order breakfast.

I choose eggs, bacon, and homemade biscuits and gravy. The biscuits are about as heavy as a brick. I slop the gravy over them. I take a taste. The roux isn't made from bacon drippings, so I am a little disappointed. I grab the hot sauce, shoot a few squirts on top and taste it again. The sauce adds a little zing. The biscuits are not done enough, though, because when I cut into the biscuits they don't crunch. If you're going to serve biscuits and gravy, at least do it right. I eat it anyway, but it sure isn't like mom's biscuits and gravy. Jon selects the steak and eggs with hash browns.

Clark orders pancakes, waffles, two orders of toast and a bran muffin. Next he tells the waitress "Hold the syrup and butter."

Jon and I just look at each other.

Leaving Wenatchee, we stop on the outskirts of town and visit Jon's brother at his work. His brother is lead mechanic for a heavy equipment repair shop. It's a short

visit with the usual greetings, conversation and picture taking.

Afterwards, we leave Wenatchee behind and get back onto Highway 97 heading north, up the eastern side of the Cascades mountains.

Then I remember, I haven't even eaten an apple yet. Here I am, in the "Apple Capital of The World", and no apple. And, no visit to the Ohme Gardens! What a bummer.

[The gardens, shown here, are high above the valley at the intersection of Hwy 2 and 97-ALT and are highly recommended. visit https://www.ohmegardens.org/ -Jon]

We're traveling North on what is called the Cascade Loop. The Loop is a beautiful scenic route over four hundred miles long and shaped like a giant oval. It goes from Seattle over the mountains to Wenatchee, north along the Cascades and then back over the mountains on Highway 20—the northern most pass in the US—then it turns South toward Seattle again onto Whidbey Island. It is one of the most scenic drives in the Pacific Northwest. Our journey will take us around three quarters of the Loop.

(More information at www.cascadeloop.com)

Jon installed a radar detector on Mabel before we left and outside of Wenatchee it comes alive, telling us we are being tracked by radar. We hear a beep, beep, beep,

on the speaker. We are within the speed limit, (One of the few times?) so we aren't busted. Still, it is nice to know when the man is watching.

We follow the Columbia River for several miles. We pass a couple of picturesque dams along the way, which make the ride interesting. One dam is the Rocky Reach Dam[18] one of Eastern Washington's major attractions.

---

[18] Visit https://www.chelanpud.org/hydropower/rocky-reach-dam

Here you can go and, using viewing windows, look a salmon in the eye as the fish make their way upstream. You can also take a self-guided tour of the Museum of Electricity. It's open year-round and if you want to picnic, park facilities are available.

We also visit the town of Chelan. It sits at the East end of Lake Chelan, which is a deep fiord-like lake that extends almost sixty miles up into the wild regions of the Cascade Mountains.

(visit **www.lakechelan.com**)

At the far end of the lake is the isolated town of Stehekin. You can't drive there, but you can hike in or take the ferry, a boat or a float plane. The lake offers steep cliffs, waterfalls, mountain goats, and yes, even an old mining town. It is quite a place for an adventure. People like to gather friends, rent a houseboat, stock it with a couple tons of foods and leisurely explore the lake. I had the impression you could take a month.

(visit https://ladyofthelake.com/   )

We turn West onto Highway 153 and start toward the Methow Valley. As we drive through the small town of Carlton, a 1952 Buick Special resting next to an old barn catches both Clark's and my attention so we stop to look at it. Clark's family had one similar to it, as did my family. Ours was a 1951 blue Buick Special with a standard shift. It was a two-door hard top, which was very stylish for the time. Four-door cars were considered family cars. I learned to drive in that beauty and had my first dates in it.

This old car brought back some fond memories. Clark and I reminisced about some of the Buick's unique features …like the starter button under the gas pedal. People, who have never driven a Buick, could never seem to get them started. It was an excellent anti-theft device. However, it wasn't often used for that as there wasn't much auto theft in those days.

We continue on, passing through the town of Twisp, and enter the Methow Valley. In the distance, towering above us are the Cascade Mountains.

Our next stop is Winthrop. It is a restored western frontier mining town in the Methow Valley[19]. We stop and do some sightseeing. We wander around town, amazed. It looks like a place straight out of the Old West. Down Main Street, there are wooden sidewalks, false-fronted buildings, and streetlights from the late 1800's. It looks like Shaniko, but with paint, and people.

In one store, Jon spies a painting he likes. It is of a trapper, who is holding on for dear life trying to calm his spooked pack horse. A blinding snowstorm is swirling all around them. From behind a large tree, a huge grizzly is standing up on its rear legs like it is ready to attack the horse and trapper. Brr, what a situation to be in.[20]

------

[19] Visit https://winthropwashington.com/ for more information

[20] This dramatic painting was above the bar at "Sam's Place" in Winthrop which, unfortunately, is no longer open.

Clark is having visions of transforming his home town of Weaverville into a place like Winthrop. He says he could make a fortune and retire someplace else.

Getting into the mood of the western town, we stumble into "3 Fingered Jacks," belly up to the bar, and hoist a few. What a warm, glowing feeling I have by the time we leave that old western saloon.

After walking up and down Main Street, we decide enough of the past let's see the present. We get into Mabel and she rumbles slowly out of town. We're looking left and right, making sure we've covered it all. Or, maybe we were looking at all the girls looking at Mabel, I forget. They have to be looking at Mabel, because they sure aren't looking at Jon and me. I check the rear-view mirror and there's Clark, 25 yards back, checking out the girls. Good idea.

We are now headed West on Highway 20. We pass through a gate made of upright logs. Etched in the high cross beam is the inscription "Gateway to The Cascades."

The Cascade Mountains[21] run from the Siskiyou Mountains in Northern California and extend northward into British Columbia where they join the Rocky Mountain chain. The Cascade Range dominates the geography of the Pacific Northwest and divides it into the semi-arid inland and damp coastal regions. On our trip North, we have been traveling through the "Inland Empire" which is the semi-arid area east of the Cascades. We've been surrounded by forests and vast, open prairie lands. Now we are headed over the mountains to visit the totally different coastal area.

---

[21] For more information visit

https://en.wikipedia.org/wiki/Cascade_Range

As we drive to the upper end of the Methow valley,
we get our first close up look at the mighty Cascades.

9 – Mountain Magic

We enter the North Cascades Highway and begin the long climb up the Cascade Mountains toward Washington Pass. It is a pretty decent climb being 5,477 feet high. But this time Mabel is keeping her cool. OK! This road, the North Cascade Highway, is one of the Nation's ten most scenic roads. I fall in love with it.

As we wind our way up the twisting roads, Jon is driving slower and slower. Finally he pulls over to the side of the road. Without a word, he gets out, walks over and sits down next to a large boulder on the cliff side of the road, and takes off his glasses. What? Are those tears I see?

He explains that these mountains are 'home' to him. He used to live just on the west side of the summit with his brothers and sisters. And this area of the North Cascades has always been home to him. He hasn't been back here in years and suddenly the experience of being here and feeling the mountains all around him just overcame him. He is so happy to be back. I wonder what he means. I haven't felt anything.

At Washington Pass, we spot a sign, "Scenic Viewpoint," and turn in. We drive to the parking area and slide Mabel into an open slot.

A paved trail leads us through the woods. A beautiful large beam fence had been built following the path. It leads us over rocks, past gullies, around trees, and up to a cliff.

This brings us to the visitors' viewpoint that overlooks the whole area. The outlook stands high on top of a huge granite boulder. Far below, we see the road we had just driven up. Across the canyon stand immense sheer cliffs stretching from the valley floor to far above our vantage point. Glaciers cling to the cliff tops high above the sloping meadows. Jon points out Liberty Bell Mountain[22]which rises far above and behind us.

There is a large graphic display that illustrates how the area had been formed. A large glacier had created the valley below by taking out massive amounts of grass, dirt, rocks, boulders, trees, and everything else in its way as it traveled. When it had finished, it had formed this magnificent valley.

Jon is excited; he's moving around, talking very fast, and eagerly pointing to this and that. Clark and I are

---

[22] See https://www.peakbagger.com/peak.aspx?pid=1918

somewhat calm. I make a comment about how the area looked like a small Yosemite Valley. Jon ignores me.

About this time, Clark asks Jon to sit still so that he can take a picture. I offer "What do you want me to do, knock him out?" A bystander, who had been watching us, drops his camera and bursts out laughing. We leave Washington Pass with fond memories.

Highway 20 now leads us slowly downhill from the Pass. The road is only ten years old, and the area is still a pristine wilderness. Here we are in the largest area of unspoiled, wild country left in the continental U.S. The scenery is immensely impressive.

As we drive through the mountains, Clark calls us on the CB. He wants us to stop for a moment. Jon pulls over to the side of the road. Clark pulls up next to us and hands Jon a cassette.

"Hey guys, you gotta hear this."

As we drive off, Jon inserts "Coming Home" by Willie Nelson into the player. The music and words slowly engulf Jon and I and there is a teary mist flowing in Mabel's wake as we drive slowly through the mountains. This is the most quiet, intensely emotional time that Jon and I share between us on the whole trip. The combination of the music and the mountains is such a powerfully beautiful experience, we just can't talk.

As we wind through the Cascades, we spot a small waterfall beside the road. We stop, climb out of the car and head straight for the waterfall. We want to cool our bodies and wash our tear streaked faces. We stand under the glistening spray highlighted by the sun. Looking up, we see sparkling, silver droplets falling towards our waiting faces. In the afternoon heat, this is heaven. Finishing our "nature shower" we continue on, wet clothes and all.

Then I have an inspiration. I tell Jon to pull over and leave me beside the road with Clark's camera. I suggest Jon and Clark drive back up the road turn and come back by me, so I can take their picture while they are in motion. Everyone agrees this would make a great photo, so I get out and they leave.

Boy, does it get quiet.

First, I notice the wind softly brushing the leaves of the trees as it pushes quietly through the forest. Then, I become aware of the mountains towering around me. I feel their massive presence descending on me. I feel their immense graceful silence surrounding me. Slowly they overpower me, and I become calm. I feel like I want to stay forever, then I feel like running away. In the silence, I'm overwhelmed by powerful, mixed emotions. Is this what Jon had felt earlier?

Where are Jon and Clark? They've been gone for over an hour. (Really, only about ten seconds.) Then I hear the oncoming sound of Mabel, rumbling her melody accompanied by Clark's Moonshadow, singing her song and the mood is broken. I try to take the picture, but I'm still feeling the mountains. I think I took it.

On we drive, stopping shortly at Ross dam overlook. As we look down at the lake, we are amazed how far below those people are, sitting in their little canoe on the beautiful sky-blue lake. It looks like a beautiful Hamm's beer commercial. Now where's that bear?

Diablo Dam is our next stop. We pull over at a scenic overlook above it. Far below, the water glows a deep emerald green. How different it is from Ross Lake we just visited a few miles back. And strange, too. We just can't figure it out. (Later we discover it is Glacier created, Granite dust mixed in the water that gives it that unique Jade green color.) Whatever the reason, it is a beautiful sight.

We drive down the road right by the entrance to the lake. Jon just keeps driving. By now, Clark and I are hungry and I have just spotted food. We tell Jon we want to stop and eat. He replies, "Okay, but first I want to show you something."

There is a small town below Diablo Dam with the same name. Before the new road was built over the pass, this was as far as you could drive up into the mountains, from the coast. Jon's brother and sisters lived in Diablo at one time and Jon used to drive up the old roads to visit them, Summer and Winter. Now, he badly wants to drive through the town again.

We enter the town of Diablo over an old bridge. It is a converted railroad bridge. A sign next to it warns that it is a one-way bridge…and it is. This little town was a company town. You could live here only if you work at the dam or power plants.

Jon drives down a few streets of very neat, clean looking homes. He parks in front of a little fire station. It's small and its style is like the other homes on the block. I think, how nice. The environmental impact agency has even reached up here, making them design the fire station to blend in with the neighborhood.

Jon corrects me and tells me that they had converted his mother's home into the fire station. Oh.

We drive toward the other end of town. On the way we see a huge inclined railroad. It is a set of tracks going right up a steep mountainside, so steep it is almost a cliff. There is a little powerhouse at the top and cables that lift an open platform up the hillside. Jon says this is how they moved all the concrete, men and material up the mountain when they built the dam back in 1928.

We go on and, reaching the end of the small town, we look around a bluff. Wow. What a sight. There, towering above us, not fifty yards away is the massive Diablo Dam. It rises hundreds of feet above us and seems to be looking right down on us. How would you like that in your back yard? What a high-tension town.

After showing us this strange town, Jon turns around and drives back up toward the food sign we'd seen on the highway. As we near the entrance, Jon slows and turns in, down a steep narrow road. Suddenly we're clinging to the side of a cliff. We hold our breath as we creep slowly forward, looking down into the deep canyon below. Finally, we are out onto the dam itself.

We drive across the top of the dam on a narrow, barely two-lane wide roadway. It resembles a bridge with a 1930s 'art deco' style. But instead, there is water on one side and a canyon on the other. Across the dam we find ourselves looking at a sign that reads "Diablo Dam Resort."

As we drive in, Jon spots a sign that says "Resort Parking" and pulls in. I suggest that maybe we should find the restaurant before we park, but Jon says that if the sign says resort parking, then we should park. So we park. Man, can he be stubborn. Clark said he would ride on and see how far the restaurant was.

Jon and I start walking but after a few minutes, Clark returns and says he had gone a half mile, with nothing in sight. Jon gives in and we return to the car and follow Clark down the road alongside the lake.

On both sides, trees crowd the road pointing up at the sky. Through the trees on the right we catch glimpses of the emerald green lake. How beautifully it complements the dark green forests and majestic mountains. However, today the lake is deserted. No boats, no one swimming, not a human being can be seen. How unusual.

We follow the road and at the end, there is a clearing. To the left a few camping sites appear in the woods. To the right, down a slope, next to the lake, hidden amongst the trees, is a large wooden building with a sign that says "Hidden Inn.[23]" Boy, is it ever well named.

---

[23] Hidden Inn and Diablo Resort no longer exist. Thus another part of history is gone. The Federal Government forced the owners out in creating an 'environmental education facility' (The North

We park and walk down the wooden steps and enter the Inn through large glass double doors. We step onto a thick carpet in a little vestibule with beautifully wood paneled walls. The hostess takes us down some more steps, through a dining room with a 25-foot-high ceiling, through another set of double doors and out onto an open deck with picnic tables and benches that overlook the emerald green lake.

We sit down and order three very cold, long neck Buds. We immediately feel at home. We decide to stay a spell. We slowly sip our beers and talk in gentle voices. The lake, the trees, the mountains, the breeze,

---

Cascades Institute) managed by the National Park service. Today you can visit but not stay unless attending an educational program. Seehttps://ncascades.org/discover/learning-center/history for the 'official' history and https://www.nps.gov/noca/index.htm for the North Cascades National Park information.

everything reaches out, and soothes us. How *peaceful* it is here.

We talk to a young lady who is sitting at a table near us. Her glazed eyes stare at the lake. She never looks at us. She tells us the water temperature is 38 degrees. (No wonder we didn't see anyone swimming in it.) It is fed by a glacier and the color was caused by minerals. Then she stops talking and just stares at the lake.

We want to eat outside but the waitress says that isn't a good idea. It would attract the bees. Big, hungry, mountain bees. We go back inside and eat.

The menu was not too extensive, and I was not too hungry. I settled for a steak sandwich and cottage cheese with peaches. Jon took a grilled ground round sandwich with some strawberries and cream.

Clark ordered a cold chicken liver sandwich. When it came, he poured catsup over it.

Jon and I just blinked…and tried not to grimace.

After a while, I turn to ask Jon a question but then I stop. Jon's eyes are all glazed over, and he is staring at the lake. Turning to Clark, I ask another question but he doesn't answer; he too is staring at the lake. After a while I hear a voice.

"What?"

The waitress replies, "I've been trying to get your attention, but you were staring at the lake."

"Oh, sorry, I didn't hear you; I was staring at the lake."

"Can I get you something else?" She wants to know.

"Yes, may I have a glass of lake?   Ahh…I mean water please."

All in all it was a fascinating, mesmerizing place.

But, at last we are out of time and have to leave. It is so difficult to pull away. We drive away looking back trying to memorize every detail. We follow the road back to Diablo dam. I ask Jon to stop the car and I get out. I want to walk across.

I borrow Clark's camera, sling it over my shoulder and start walking slowly across the dam. I can really feel the massive size of this great structure of steel and concrete. As I approach mid span I stop, lean way over the edge and take a picture of the canyon far below. Wow, very far below.

Hanging over the edge like that, I become somewhat apprehensive and I start getting visions of the whole thing letting go and me ending up in Hawaii. I straighten up and quickly walk away.

When I safely reach the other side, I whistle to Jon and Clark. They drive slowly across the dam. As they near me, I take some quick pictures. They drive on by

and park. As I walk up to the car, I turn around, wave goodbye and silently thank the dam for not sending me to Hawaii. Then we drive off leaving Diablo Dam behind, all the while making silent promises to ourselves to return and explore this magical place.

We drive on, twisting and turning through the mountains and enjoying the view. It is a beautiful time.

For more information about the Diablo Dam visit https://www.seattle.gov/light/damtours/skagit.asp.

Mabel (you do remember Mabel?) evidently began to feel like she was being ignored. After all, everyone has been paying attention to the mountains and not her. So, she started to pout. Then, when that didn't get her any attention, she decided to eat her generator.

The first indication we have that something is wrong is when the generator light starts blinking. Finally, it comes on and stays on. We are still travelling in daylight so Jon feels we can make it a little farther on the battery.

We stop at Rockport where Jon checks the generator circuit over while Clark and I drop into the local pub and have a long neck Bud. It is so refreshing. Finally, Jon joins us and reports that he can't fix the generator. That is not so refreshing. We finish our beer and get back into Mabel. Jon starts the engine and we drive slowly out of town watching the glowing generator light. At the junction of Highway 20 we turn west and head for Sedro-Woolley.

Along the way, we stop in the little town of Concrete where Jon had attended a year of Grade school. It had been a strange change for him as he had already graduated Grade school and had finished seventh grade in North Jr. High School in his home town (now known as 'Middle school'—sometimes, I really think the school system is retrogressing).

Then he had moved to Rockport where he graduated from 8th grade in grade school again because their system was different (Eight years of grade school and four years of high school).

After that he had returned to Everett where he graduated from the 9^{th}grade in South Jr. High School— all before he entered high school. So unlike most kids, he graduated four times before he ever went to college.

As we drive by, we also see Concrete's High School that his siblings had attended (and where he would have gone had he stayed in Rockport). They have built the school elevated above the road. When you drive up to the school, you actually drive under the school building to reach the front door. It is quite an unusual sight.

Driving down out of the mountains through Skagit Valley has many beautiful vistas. The valley takes its name from the large river that flows through it, starting deep in the Cascades on its way out to the Pacific Ocean. The lowest part is flat and fertile having been nourished by the river for thousands of years. Here, hundreds of acres of colorful tulips and daffodils paint the landscape during early spring. The tulip crop here is the new world's largest. With the picturesque barns and azure skies as a background, photographers swarm here to capture the blazing fields of brilliant color during the internationally famous Tulip Festival in April. Even when the Tulips are not blooming, it is a beautiful place.

The Upper valley is bordered by large, forest covered mountains. For decades logging was the main industry in this heavily forested area. We roll into Sedro-Woolley, home of the Logger's Rodeo, finally ending our day of adventure.

The generator light is still glowing, but Mabel has brought us to our next destination. This is where Jon's mom, Winnie Martin lives and works. Clark and I are both welcomed with open arms. She has long heard of me and has been anxious to finally meet me in person. She kind of makes me feel like I'm famous.

As we'd previously arranged, it's time for Clark to leave us and continue on his personal journey to see some of other friends and visit other places. We make plans to meet up with him on Thursday morning at the

Anacortes Ferry Landing. There we will continue our trip to the San Juan Islands. After that he will be off to see Victoria and the Washington Peninsula. [See Chapter 12 for Clark's story of his adventures]

Later that evening we drive Mabel into his mom's garage and begin to work on her. We remove the generator. Jon notes that it smells burned. As he tilts it sideways to look inside, some pieces fall out and go scattering across the floor.

"Oh shucks," Jon comments.

"Oh dear," I agree.

Jon disassembles the rest of the generator. It looks bad. (With parts of it all over the floor, I didn't think things could get worse.) Jon kindly translates the technical problem in terms I can understand.

"The thing-a-ma-jig has worn out the what-cha-ma-call-it."

It's clear that Mabel's generator is broke beyond repair. We are dead in the water.

Jon goes back into his Mom's house and starts to make some phone calls looking for parts—namely a generator for a 1955 XK140 Jaguar. (Like they grow on trees, right.)

Amazingly, he strikes pay dirt. He has a brother-in-law, Phil, who lives in Seattle (only about 80 miles away) who is well acquainted with automotive parts stores. He has found a rebuilt generator, exactly Mabel's type, sitting on a shelf in a parts store in Seattle and he has given Jon the address. All we have to do is drive to Seattle tomorrow, pick it up, come back and put it in. Winnie offers to let us use her car and thus we have a plan to put us back in action. So finally, I can stop worrying.

Jon and I go to bed at a reasonable hour--which really means past midnight. After all, we had a lot to talk with Jon's mom about and he and I just have to go through the family album. I am getting to know my friend a lot better.

As I twist and turn trying to get to sleep, I think about poor Mabel. Already, she's run out of breath, got hot and bothered twice, thrown a shoe, and now she's lost her spark.

It makes it difficult to fall asleep. I keep thinking about what unknown perils may lay ahead.

10 – The Peace Arch and My Town, USA

Tuesday morning finds us rested and, after a quick, home-made breakfast, ready for our side trip into Seattle. We clean up, climb into Winnie's car and drive South. The drive down I-5 is uneventful. We find the store and acquire the generator without any unexpected problems. With the exception of the usual city traffic (I had forgotten what it was like, having acres of cars around me pushing and shoving.) we are back in Sedro-Woolley in what seems like a fairly short time.

Jon dives under Mabel's bonnet and starts twisting wrenches. In a short time, he has the generator installed. He fires Mabel up and then, just as quickly, shuts her back off.

The ammeter needle has pinned to the *minus side* of the gauge. Mabel's new generator is discharging the battery instead of charging it.

"Oh Dear," I think. "Not again. What is wrong now?"

Jon analyzes the situation and says that the polarity on the new generator's field windings is reversed. (the what-cha-ma-thingy is in backwards?) While this sounds bad, (Uh, huh!) Jon says it is easy to fix. (Oh, really?) We can re-polarize the generator. (…and just how are we going to do that? It sounds complicated…and expensive) Jon strips insulation from an old lamp cord, wires it to the battery and taps it against the generator's field terminal. (What is this?… Some kind of magic? …or guesswork?)

Jon restarts the engine and, sure enough, the ammeter needle goes positive. (What? Wow! Genius!) Everything is working fine again. We are hot!

We repack our tools in Mabel and go wash up. All this time Winnie has been having a women's club meeting. Since we're there, working on Mabel, we are invited to join them for a buffet luncheon. But by the time we join them; they have finished lunch and are beginning their meeting. However, they insist that we have something to eat anyway. So Jon and I heap our plates with lots of lunch meat, potato salad, macaroni salad, casseroles, rolls, desserts, and things I don't recognize. But it all tastes just fine.

Now, I am a little nervous sitting there among all these ladies I don't know, so I eat a little fast so we can hurry and get out of here. Not Jon. He is just slowly munching away, enjoying his food, talking and taking all the time in the world. He's a slow eater anyway, but right now he is really slow. I think he's doing that on purpose. He knows I'm jittery. He likes doing things like that to me. At last Jon finishes. We excuse ourselves and go pack our clothes for the trip.

Just as I am getting into the car, Jon stops me. He wants to take one last picture of his mom and me. I crack her up with a slightly off-color remark just as Jon snaps the picture. It turns out to be a great picture.

Now, at last we're off to more new adventures.

Canada here we come. As we drive north from Sedro-Woolley, imaginary pictures of Canada flash through my mind. I've always had a desire to visit Canada and at long last I'm going to get to do it...even though we are only going to be just stepping across the border.

I become more excited as we approach the border and start swiveling my head from side to side. My eyeballs just won't keep still. It is a very beautiful area and I am not in the least disappointed.

In Blaine, we pull over and stop at a park with a large totem pole and a sign explaining the history of the area.

"Hey, Everett. Follow me; I want to show you something." Jon is already out of the car walking across the park.

I follow Jon down a large grassy hill and across a road. There, between two roads, in the middle of a huge green lawn stands a large white structure.

It is in the shape of an arch at least 50 feet high. (I find out later that it is 67 feet high, built of reinforced concrete and steel and reputed to be the first earthquake proof structure in North America.)

"Come on inside," coaxes Jon.

I step inside the arch. The shade is cool. I look around me. I see the green grass and the blue water of Puget Sound. White puffy clouds dot the sky to the North. Jon and I stand there in silence for a long time.

"Step right here." Jon whispers to me.

I step over to where he indicated.

"You are now standing in both the United States *and* Canada."

I look down for some sign or line. But it is just grass.

"No Everett, you won't find a marker. You are standing inside the Peace Arch which separates the two countries. To the West you see Puget Sound. To the East lies the longest undefended border in the world. It is shared by the United States and Canada."

"Wow." I admit. I'm impressed.

"Notice the inscriptions above you. One on the Canadian side and one on the American side. They are such beautiful thoughts and they hold such hope for the future. Stand here and I'll take your picture."

He takes my picture standing inside the Arch with a big stupid grin. I am really happy. Later, we walk around and look at the different displays. I feel very moved to think that two countries can be so open to each other. I really like Canada.

(See http://www.peacearchpark.org/   )

Finally, we leave the Peach Arch Park and head south for Bellingham. Jon wants to do something special. As a young boy, he had often visited his Grandfather's house in Bellingham. Now, as a grown man, he'd like to see it again.

We find the house easily and Jon gets out and sits down on the steps leading to the house. I take a picture and we leave. Jon is very moved by this simple, little old house and the experience of revisiting it.

"Please try to understand, Everett," Jon tells me as we drive away, "I first saw this house when I was two years old, and my mother and father were a young married couple, struggling and poor. My dad had just entered the Navy and was about to be shipped overseas in WWII. My mother came from a large, poor farming family and she thought my father's family were rich. So from the time I was very small, I always believed this was the huge home of my rich grandparents. As a little boy, it always seemed so large and luxurious to me."

"Today, I look at this little old house and I am

amazed to find how small it actually is. So many memories are bound up in it. But now that my grandparents have died, and my parents have gone their separate ways, I find that when I look at it—at my own past—through adult eyes, I get a very different perspective. I see that things are really different from what I thought they were, growing up." Jon was silent for quite a while after that.

We stop for gas in Bellingham and Mabel, once again, is the star of the show. Everyone in the station crowds around her and asks the same questions. "How fast will it go?" "What year is it?" "How much is it worth?" "Can we see the engine?" All this attention to Mabel brings Jon back to life.

When they ask about the engine, he always obliges. He pulls the hood release, walks to the front of Mabel, trips the safety catch, and then slowly raises the hood. (American for "bonnet")

It is like unveiling the crown jewels, as Mabel has a beautifully painted and detailed engine. First, the polished aluminum cam covers come into sight. Next, the polished brass parts shine and sparkle like gold nuggets. And finally, jutting out from the engine on the passenger's side comes the "Piece de Resistance". Three huge, aluminum domed SU carburetors, all polished and gleaming, accompanied by a chorus of shiny, diamond-like chrome linkages, levers, golden brass nuts on chrome washers with black water and red fuel lines snaking throughout.

Mouths always drop open and "Gee" and "Wow" are the only comments. Mabel's engine room gets 'em every time.

Back on the highway we search for the north end of a coast road called Chuckanut Drive. Jon spots the exit and we enter a tree-covered lane lined with beautiful homes. As we continue on, the homes are replaced by woods on the left, and on the right, a very large body of water. It looks like a large bay.

"Everett, this is the northern part of Puget Sound."

Well I had heard of Puget Sound, but I hadn't imagined it being so large. From what I know, the Puget Sound starts at the capital city, Olympia, sixty miles below Seattle. But here we are up near Bellingham, a good ninety miles North of Seattle and he says this is *also* Puget Sound? Whew.

We stop to take pictures and appreciate the view. Jon points across the open waters to what appears to me to be gray lumps on the distance horizon.

"Well Everett, there's the San Juan Islands. That's where we're going Thursday morning"

"Why?"

"My sister lives there."

"Why?" I ask again.

"You'll see." He smiles…

They just look like gray lumps in the distance to me. I am not very impressed by them. But Jon seems excited.

Must be something I'm missing, so I look again. I see the same thing, gray lumps in the distance. Maybe when I get there I might see things differently, but at the moment, I just give Jon a questioning look.

He smiles like he knows something I don't.

Chuckanut Drive[24] turns out to be a beautiful, two-lane twisting road along the edge of Puget Sound, bordered by mountains on our left and views of the Islands on our right. At one time, this was the only road connecting Bellingham with Seattle and the rest of America. This is because the Cascade Mountains come right down into the waters of the Pacific Ocean at this one point, forming a natural barrier that separates Bellingham from the rest of the state. For all of the hundreds of miles that the Cascades form the backbone of both Washington and Oregon, this is the only place they actually cross over and reach the ocean.

We enjoy the scenic drive alongside the rocky cliff faces and forested mountains, overlooking the beautiful bays and islands. Even though it is a relatively short distance of about eight miles, it rivals the best of the better known scenic drives in America.

After leaving Chuckanut Drive we get back on I-5 and drive South toward the city where we plan to spend the night. Jon takes the exit leading to the north end of town and finally, we approach the city limits of his home town, Everett, Washington.

---

[24] Visit https://www.visitskagitvalley.com/chuckanut-drive

The local Budweiser distributors have placed a very large billboard alongside the road. There, in letters at least six feet high, it announces to the world...

"*EVERETT*, This Bud's for YOU!"

WOW! I was so shocked; I almost fell out of the car!

As we enter town, I really feel at home. My name is everywhere I look. There is the Everett Fire Department, the Everett Dry Cleaners, the Everett Pawn Shop, even a street named Everett. There is the Everett Library, and the Everett Motor movies, and even, (ahumph), The Bank of Everett. (For more see https://everettwa.gov/)

Jon takes me through downtown, and shows me the local High School, yep, it's Everett High School. (also known as the "School of Champions") He says that this high school has a history of winning that stretches back to the 1920s when it won its first national football championship. Really!

Now, if you've always lived with a name that is not at all common, and you get thrown into a place where *all you see* is *your name*, you get a little *giddy*.

My mind goes back to the first day I met Jon. I remember shaking hands with him and introducing myself.

"Hi, I'm Everett. You probably won't remember my name." It was my usual introductory comment.

Jon had glanced at me with a surprised look—and a smile had slowly spread over his face. "Are you kidding?" he had said, "I'll never forget it. It's where I grew up."

Back then, it was a quizzical reply that I had not understood. When all other people I met had trouble remembering my name, he picked it up immediately. And now that I've finally seen Jon's hometown, I understand why. I am very happy. After all these years, I understand why we've been such close friends. (I feel more at home here than he would ever believe.)

Afterwards, as we drive to his father's home, Jon shows me the Junior High School he had attended and especially the spot where the students used to catch the bus to go home. He tells me that in order to get into shape; he had started racing the bus home -- on foot.

Although he always had a head start, he points out how far he had run the first day before the bus caught him. It was about four blocks. As we travel, Jon explains how, each day he ran, he had gotten a little farther before the bus overtook him. Finally, after weeks of continually trying, he was able to beat the bus all the way home.

I've been watching the odometer and the distance is over two miles. And it isn't flat ground either. There are three good hills and valleys along the way. And the hills are very steep. I admire his accomplishment. Not being a runner, I would have been found alongside the road dead, if I had tried something like that.

We arrive at Jon's parents' house. Don and Kathleen are home. Kathleen is recovering from a recent surgery and is moving very slowly. Their house sits on a hill, overlooking the Port of Everett (Port Gardner Bay). You can see Mt. Baker in the distance. Don had built his home in the fifties with high ceilings and exposed beams. It is so open. You have room to breathe. I really like their home. However, we had arrived too late to share dinner, so, after introductions, we leave and drive to Mukilteo.

At Mukilteo we have dinner at Taylor's Landing[25], a little restaurant sitting on the dock right over the water and right next to the ferry landing. I have a combination seafood dish. It has an interesting variety of sea life which I do not recognize, prepared in some strange way. I eat it anyway[26].

Jon tells me we might see a ferry.

Big deal. I've seen plenty of ferries growing up in the delta country in central California. They are cable-drawn, they hold four cars and a small dog. If the cable breaks, you drift for days. Ferries are nothin'.

While we are eating dinner, a ferry does come in and starts to unload. As I was watch, two cars and then a big

---

[25] Taylor's Landing is now being run by Ivar's, highly Recommended. Visit https://www.ivars.com/locations/mukilteo-landing

[26] Tourists today will find the cuisine at Ivar's to be excellent. Everett just wasn't used to seafood. JR

eighteen-wheeler come rolling off. Then several dozen more cars, a group of motorcycles, and more than a few huge motor homes come rolling out of the hole in the front of that ferry. For fifteen minutes they drive past the restaurant's window and disappear into the darkness. Whoa! That is the largest ferry I have ever seen.

We leave Taylor's Landing fat and happy. As we pull away from the curb, we hear a crunch and the tinkle of breaking glass. Jon stops, backs up and I look down on the ground. There is my flattened hat and broken sun glasses. In my opening the door to get in, they had fallen out and I hadn't seen them.

"Oh heck," I blurt out.

"Oh dear," Jon mutters.

Mabel doesn't say anything. (Mischievous girl, I think she is grinning.)

That night, we decide to go and visit Jon's first fiancée, Bonnie. We have a very pleasant visit. Bonnie pulls out a photo album and we all get a chuckle out of looking at photographs (which are over 20+ years old.) of very young, teenaged Jon and Bonnie. Why, he'd even had hair. Red Hair?! Bonnie and Jon reminisce about all the good times they'd had when they were young and together. We have a lot of laughs that evening. I am learning more about my friend. Not too many people I know are on such good terms with their first loves—especially after being apart so many years.

We drive back to Don and Kathleen's home and crash for the night. The next morning, I ask Kathleen if she would like a little massage and she winces. I tell her to relax, as I will work on her arm and feet only. After a half hour, I have her very relaxed and very comfortable. She is amazed at how much it helps.

===================== ==================

Next morning is Wednesday and overcast. After a cup of coffee, we fire Mabel up and start our drive to Seattle. As we leave Don's house and drive toward town, Jon goes to shift into fourth gear, but it won't go.

"Ah shucks," said Jon.

"Oh dear," I add.

He slows down, shifts to second, then third, and tries fourth again. No luck. After several more tries Jon finally manages to get it into fourth by pulling very hard. Later, after the transmission warms up, the problem disappears, but we're still a little concerned about it. I wonder if the earlier incident with the transmission outside Antelope, Oregon had done some damage after all. I hope not.

We drive to Snohomish to visit Jon's sister, Judy. But she is not at home.

"We'll just go see my other sister, Nancy." (How many sisters does this guy have?)

We drive through north Seattle's winding streets and slowly climb small grades, ending up in front of a small looking house. A cute, short brunette comes running out and greets Jon with a big, warm hug. I get a handshake. (I would have taken a hug, too.)

Nancy is a wonderful hostess. I get the guided tour through a most interesting home. Nancy and her husband, Phil, have been building on the original structure for several years and I can't believe how large it is inside. (Yes, Phil is the one who found us the new generator for Mabel.) There are several floors with stairs leading you to different parts of the house. I got lost.

Phil has a large garage built under the house. It is a tinker's dream. It has all the room in the world to build anything you want.

Nancy shows us their bedroom that she had decorated herself. I love it. A thick white carpet covers about an acre of floor. What a large room. Everything is in soft colors and is frilly and nice. A real woman's touch. The house is like a miniature Winchester home.

With some regret, we tell Nancy we have to be on our way because of our tight schedule. We say our goodbyes and leave.

We drive down Highway 99 past Green lake, by the edge of Woodland Park, and across the George Washington Memorial Bridge. The locals call it "The Ballard Bridge." It's also locally known, infamously, as a lover's leap. Looking over the bridge's edge, down more than 20 stories, I can see why. We pass Queen Anne Hill, and lo and behold, there is the *Space Needle*. It is

60 stories high and looks like a futuristic Saucer, spinning on a tall, curving pole.

I can't wait to get to the top.

Seattle Center is home of the *Space Needle* and many other attractions that were built during the 1962 Seattle World's Fair. As we walk through the Center, Jon points out the different buildings and what they were used for. At the *Space Needle* we want to have lunch in the restaurant, but the wait is two hours to get a seat, so we just go to the observation deck. He takes a picture of me standing back, way back, from the rail but I'll treasure it. We walk around the observation deck, look at the view of Seattle, and down we come. It was a memorable experience for me. Jon was ho-hum about it. [I didn't know Ev was so nervous about heights until we looked over the edge of the needle. We are both learning about each other. Jon]

(See https://www.spaceneedle.com/)

We are still hungry for lunch, so Jon takes me to the greatest little place to eat. It is *The Iron Horse Restaurant* in downtown Seattle. The menu is limited, but our lunch is delivered by a model train. It comes balanced on a flat car pulled by an early 1900's engine and coal car with the inscription "B & O Railroad" on its side.

All during our lunch we hear trains steaming by, tooting their whistles and ringing their bells as they hurry to serve hot lunches to other hungry people. I am tempted to snatch some food off a passing flat car, but I can just see myself derailing a bowl of hot soup onto Jon's lap. So I refrain from making a fool of myself. It's really an enjoyable lunch.[27]

Another reason we are in downtown Seattle is to visit underground Seattle, "The Forgotten City Which Lies Beneath Seattle's Modern Streets."[28] The building of this underground city has a strange history. Seattle was originally built on soft marshy tidelands. They continued struggling with the problem for years. After the great fire in 1889 the city fathers rebuilt the downtown. They raised the streets because, when the tide came in, water

---

[27] The Iron Horse Restaurant closed Nov. 10, 2000 (https://archive.seattletimes.com/archive/?date=20001122&slug=TTNA2DPP4)

[28] Visit https://en.wikipedia.org/wiki/Seattle_Underground

and mud flooded into the streets, homes and buildings. Eventually, the streets had been raised a full one story high, leaving the sidewalks and the store fronts below. People were being hurt falling off the street onto the sidewalk (Imagine that.) so eventually they covered the sidewalks over.

Now, you can go underground on a tour and walk the original sidewalks and see the original store fronts that survived the fire long ago.

During the prohibition era this area had been used as storage for booze and other 'less than legal' enterprises. Because it is out of the weather, hobos used it as winter homes. The local store owners also used it for storage. Today, it has been cleaned up for tourists to visit. Walking the original sidewalks and looking up at people walking overhead through glass sidewalk holes, oblivious to the life below, is an interesting experience. It is a very mysterious place.

We leave downtown Seattle and head north to Bothell to visit our friends, Tom, Donna, Tommy and Noel. Tom and his family had moved from the bay area eight years previously. It is good to see our friends again. We sit around and reminisce about old times until once again my stomach yells "Feed Me" "Feed Me."

So we all get up and go to a nice Mexican restaurant and have a wonderful dinner. We later go to their friend's house and sit nose deep in a wonderful hot tub. We let our tired bodies get pounded by a million or so tiny bubbles. Ahhhh…. This is a great end to a day of visiting friends, relatives and strange places.

Later that night, I put my head onto a soft pillow and fall gently into a deep sleep.

11 – Trials and Beauty

Thursday morning comes quite early. Today, we have quite a drive. We are going to Anacortes, an old sea-faring city, resting at the water's edge on Fidalgo Island. Anacortes is a small, artsy town that has a lot of nautical connections, be it fishing, ship building or the many yachts that grace her beautiful harbor. From there we will catch a ferry to the San Juan Islands where another of his sisters lives. We have to be on time to catch the ferry.

We head north, up Highway 5, in the chilly morning air. We turn off the freeway and head West on highway 20 toward Anacortes and the ferry landing. We are just coming into Anacortes when all of a sudden the road becomes very rough. It feels like a vibrator. I look ahead and the road looks smooth to me.

Jon asks, "Do you feel that?"

"Yep." I shake my head sadly.

"Oh fiddlesticks." says Jon.

"Oh heck." I respond.

Jon slows down and the rear end feels as if it wants to jump into the air. Yep, Mabel has thrown another shoe. Jon is upset.

"I don't understand this," he says, "I put brand new tires on the car when I started to restore her, and they don't have more than a few thousand miles on them. ...of course that was a few years ago. You don't think sitting in the garage all those years damaged them, do you?"

I feel sick. I am thinking of my wild slide avoiding that car in Eastern Washington. And what about Clark's statement about only having one flat per trip? I wish he was here now, to discuss the matter.

Jon wants to keep moving at a slower speed and see if we can make it to the ferry in time. After all, we're almost there. If we miss the ferry we will have a long wait for the next one and that will really limit our stay on the island.

We bump along the road and worry. We keep looking at the mileage and the time as we slowly limpity-bump our way through Anacortes toward the ferry.[29] It seems to take *forever*. Then, with just minutes to spare, we spy the ferry landing. We've *just* made it.

We stop at the toll booth, and Jon buys our ticket. We are told to go to lane 2. We bump down a long asphalt drive and see a series of numbers mounted high above the lanes. We move over to lane 2 and stop behind a car pulling a boat. We get out to stretch and unwind. Who do we see at the front of the line next to us? Clark!

---

[29] For information on Washington State Ferries, see https://www.wsdot.wa.gov/ferries/

It's good to see him and Moonshadow safe and sound. After handshakes and greetings, we tell him about the tire.

He starts to tell us about the statistics of three flat tires happening on the same trip but suddenly stops. Maybe it is the lug wrench I am holding in my hand, swinging slowly back and forth by my side? Am I threatening my good friend Clark? Nooooo, not me!

The ferryman signals that it is loading time. Jon and I climb into Mabel. I watch Clark take off. Jon starts the engine and we follow the traffic moving slowly down a slight incline and onto the ferry. A crewman directs us to the left and up a ramp to the second level. Then we follow a long corridor and, at the direction of another crewman, stop behind a station wagon. The crewman walks by us to direct the car following us. As we are getting out, Clark joins us from the front of the line. Motorcycles get privileges.

Following the large signs and arrows, we make our way to an upper, enclosed deck. They even have a cafeteria and a large lounge on board. Jon asks Clark and I not to eat here though, because he has plans to have a special breakfast once we get on the island.

"Jon, do you mind if I have a cup of coffee? Please?" I plead.

"Yes, you may"

(If he had said "No" I would have keel hauled him.)

Jon and Clark join me for coffee which we have in the lounge. It was our first food of the day. It's just coffee but it is wonderful.

I am waiting to feel the deep throbbing

throughout the vessel and the lurch backward from the dock indicating we are on our way.

I am wondering what is taking so long, so I glance out the window. I am surprised to see the shore line moving by. We have already left the dock and I haven't even felt the movement. I think what a smooth and quiet vessel.

I step onto the deck outside. The warm morning sun hits my face and a fresh sea breeze brushes against me. I walk up front and watch the bow cut through the deep blue green water, throwing splashes of white spray aside. We are gliding smoothly in a westerly direction toward those gray lumps.

This is Rosario Strait, one of the many waterways through the San Juan Islands. Natives, who think of Puget Sound as a jewel, consider the San Juan Islands to be her brightest facets. They would probably be upset to hear me refer to them as "gray lumps."

I turn my head into the wind to get a whiff of the salt air but guess what? No salt smell. It is just very clean, fresh air. I turn and see Clark and Jon. What smiles. I look around and see everyone is smiling. We are really enjoying the trip.

We see floating objects and Jon points at the gray lumps in the distance and gives them names.

"That's Lopez. That's Orcas. No, it's not, that must be Blakely. Where's Orcas? Let's see if Lopez is there, then... then..." I knew it, we are lost.

A bird floating on a large piece of wood watches us carefully as we move slowly by and then rides our wake to the crest and down the other side. He is looking back as if to say "Hey, can we do that again"?

I put a quarter in a telescope and watch the shoreline and islands passing by. Each island is sparsely populated by small buildings and boat docks. Near them, they have everything from outboards to large cruisers bobbing slowly up and down. Each island looks like the top of a large steep mountain. This is definitely not like the high, flat plains of Eastern Washington and Oregon.

We move quietly and smoothly in wide arcs as the pilot negotiates our passage through the San Juan Islands.

I feel like I am on a flying carpet gliding through a magic kingdom. I can hardly wait to zoom high into the sky and fly through the large clouds floating gently above us.

I feel a slight slowing down and look up. In the distance, I see a ferry docking and loading cars. After a few minutes, it backs away from the dock, stops, and then turning around, passes us on the left. It is like watching ourselves from a distance.

We move slowly toward the dock. Mounted high above the dock, on two large poles, is a sign that reads "Lopez Island." [30]

The ferry glides smoothly into the dock and stops just before hitting it. Two men jump off each side of the loading ramp onto the dock and throw large ropes with loops in them, around stanchions. Somewhere a winch, which we don't see, tightens the ropes. The ramp is lowered and cars move off the ferry, up an incline and down a paved road out of sight.

---

[30] For more information, visit https://lopezisland.com/

Off to the side, a man waves his hand and two cars and a large truck move down the incline, onto the ferry and out of sight below us. The two crewmen move quickly to the stanchions, remove the now loose ropes and heave them aboard. And then, after they've secured the ropes, they run up the loading ramp. The ramp is raised and we move smoothly away from the dock, leaving a wake of white, churning water behind us.

Of all the ferries I rode, the unloading and loading was always just as smooth and fast.

We're approaching another ferry landing and Jon is starting to get anxious.

"That's where we're going," he says.

I read the sign over the approaching landing and it says "Orcas Island".[31] At last, we have arrived at our destination. All of us are high with anticipation. We try to be casual walking to the vehicles, but you can't help but see the little skip in our step.

We get into Mabel, Jon starts her engine and then we notice—Mabel is running very rough. It sounds like Mabel isn't running on all cylinders. I get a whiff of gasoline. She coughs and staggers as she struggles to pull away. I look back and see a small puddle of gasoline on the deck of the ferry.

"Oh poop," I remark.

I mention the puddle to Jon, but he is concentrating on keeping Mabel running, so he isn't looking back. It looks like Mabel has gotten seasick and tossed her

---

[31] For more information visit https://orcasislandchamber.com/

cookies. I guess Mabel, being feline, doesn't like riding ferries as much as we do.

We struggle up the loading ramp. Jon quickly pulls into a parking place at the nearby Orcas Hotel. Clark pulls up and parks next to us. He starts looking at his watch, shakes his head and yawns.

"Stop that," I yell. He looks hurt, and then grins.

We get out. Jon opens the hood and I start looking around. I feel the carburetors. The one next to the fire wall is as wet as a baby's bottom. It is covered with gasoline and dripping the excess on the ground. I relay the information to Jon and he turns off the engine. However, since we haven't had breakfast yet, he decides to eat first and then look at the problem.

As it turns out, the hotel serves a fantastic, delicious breakfast. Again I have eggs, bacon and this time, rolls. The coffee is very good. Jon is into steak and eggs again.

I don't listen to what Clark orders, and I avoid looking at what he's eating. It is too nice of a day to get into that.

The waitress asks Jon if he is Sea-ell's brother. Jon answers "Yes." (As least, now I know her name. Sea-ell, huh? That's a strange name.) I guess that, on a small island, everyone knows what is going on. No one is a stranger.

After breakfast, Jon takes the carburetor apart, does some of his magic and reassembles it. He fires up the engine. Mabel runs very smoothly. I feel all around the carburetor, and it is dry. Mabel is purring on all six cylinders again. What a relief. Jon has been so calm about it. My earlier feelings of trust are confirmed. He can fix anything.

It is now late morning as we drive into the island. Orcas Island is roughly shaped like a big horseshoe with the ferry landing on the lower left arm of the shoe. Our destination is the little village of Eastsound which is located at the middle of the island between the two arms. We pull into Eastsound and discover it borders the most beautiful bay. We rest a tranquil moment and just view the islands offshore.

After a few moments reflection we turn around, head up Main Street and stop at a building with a sign that says, "The Hair Company."

We go inside. There Clark and I meet Jon's sister, Carolyn. (Huh? I thought her name was Sea-ell?)

Immediately, both Clark and I fall in love.

"Carolyn," I get her attention. "I thought your name was Sea-ell."

"CL," she answers. "It's what the locals call me, but you may call me Carolyn." (I would have called her anything she wanted.)

Carolyn is very glad to see us as she's heard on the news about fires in northern California disrupting traffic. So, it's hugs and kisses for Jon and handshakes for Clark and me. (I think she held Clark's hand longer than mine.)

Carolyn owns "The Hair Company," so she can't leave work just now. She says we can stay at her place until she gets off work, so we borrow her keys and drive over to her house. I am tired and I need a nap but Jon is concerned about Mabel needing tires (After all, poor Mabel is still limpity-bumping along.). So he drives off to find some tires.

Clark leaves too. He wants to go sightseeing. [see chapter 12]

I find a nice soft couch and a warm blanket and fall immediately to sleep. I must have slept for an hour or so. When I awake, I am still alone. I get up and decide to take a walk to see some of the island. I find a small harbor with little boats. It looks so very quaint. I follow a trail through some woods, keeping an eye out for snakes. (I don't like the rush they give me.) I walk down a paved road that runs through a thick forest. Orcas Island has a little of everything. [Except snakes. -Jon]

When I return an hour later, Clark and Carolyn are just pulling up, Carolyn in her car and Clark on Moonshadow. We go into the house and spend some time getting to know one another.

We are still talking when Jon returns with two new rear tires on Mabel. He says he is really happy he found them. They are not exactly the same make, style, or size but he says that they will be good enough to get us home[32]. I trust his judgment. Mabel is completely well again.

---

[32] Jon: The tires were for a larger series Volkswagen, which I elected not to tell Everett. The ribbing Mabel and I would have gotten wouldn't be worth it. Besides, when one is choosing tires at the only supplier, in a small village, on an island, one has to be flexible. Mabel would have to make the rest of the trip on two black walls and two whitewalls...more about that later.

Later in the evening we have a great Mexican dinner at Bilbo's and go bar hopping. Between bars, Carolyn convinces Jon to let her drive Mabel. I convince him I should go with her. I believe the drinks must have made him an old softy. Carolyn gets into the driver's seat. I show her how to start Mabel, what the shift pattern is, and tell her that, under no circumstances, is she to flip the switch with the red light on the dash board.

She drives carefully out of the parking lot and turns north. I look in my rear-view mirror and see Clark behind us. Here, I finally get Carolyn alone, and before I know it, I have a chaperone. Darn. I look again and see Jon hanging on behind Clark. Double darn, two chaperones and one is her brother.

Carolyn handles the car without a bit of difficulty. In fact, she does a lot better than I did the first time I took Mabel for a spin. As we turn here and there, Carolyn asks why the turn signals don't work. I thought they were working. She insists, "No, they don't." I check and sure enough they don't work. (Maybe Mabel is sensitive about women driving her?)

We stop at the Inn where Carolyn occasionally tends bar. It seems you have to work at several jobs to survive on the island. We have a few drinks and a very nice time visiting. When we leave the bar, Jon and I take Mabel and, as we are driving, I mention the turn signal problem.

He tries them several times and then mumbles something I don't quite hear. I think it sounded like "Oh fudge."

We park at a beach near Smuggler's Villa. We walk around the beach in the sand and rocks. I sit down on a large boulder and watch a large multicolored sunset unfold over the Straits of Georgia. Ships can be seen making their way through the straits heading for some port in Canada. Other ships are making their way out to sea, destination unknown. The night is warm, and the world is very peaceful. It is beautiful.

I could have stayed on the beach all night.

We get back to Carolyn's house late and everyone goes to bed. Jon and I take the couches, Clark gets the floor, and Carolyn disappears some place in back of the house.

As I drift off to sleep, I dream again about Mabel. She's run out of breath, lathered twice, thrown two shoes, lost her spark, jammed up her box, gotten seasick, and lost her direction, but so far, *she hasn't stranded us*. I don't know whether to hate her or love her.

Morning comes early again. Carolyn has to go to work, and Clark is leaving us to go to Canada. He says he will try and meet us in Portland the next day. [See Chapter 12 for Clark's story of his adventures.]

They leave and Jon and I stumble around the house until we can see. Jon tells me not to take a shower because the summer's unusually long drought has caused a water shortage on the island. (Now that's strange. All I've heard about Washington is its rain, rain, rain. I get here, and they're having a drought?) We pack our gear in Mabel and leave Carolyn's home.

We go through Eastsound and drive down a road that parallels the shore and leads to the east side of the island. We pass a sign that reads "Rosario Resort."[33] Jon says we will stop there for breakfast on the way back.

We continue on, entering Moran State Park.[34] I wonder who this guy Moran was. We cross an old steel-concrete bridge and climb up a twisty road that leads us through a deep forest. The road takes us higher and higher. After several miles we find ourselves on top of a mountain, Mt. Constitution. A mountain on an island?

We park and walk up a path that winds through the woods. It leads us to a stone and wood lookout tower on top of the mountain. The tower had been a CCC project in the thirties.

There, the stones for the tower had been quarried, loaded aboard a barge, floated over to Orcas to a dock, loaded aboard trucks, and then hauled up the steep mountain roads to this spot. Here, the craftsmen had shaped and moved the large stones into place, building this 12th century style watch tower.

---

[33] Visit https://rosarioresort.com/

[34] Visit http://www.thesanjuans.com/orcas-island-places/orcas-parks-forest/orcas-islands-moran-state.shtml

It must have been quite an undertaking.

It has a beautiful panoramic view. I look to the North and see Sucia Island. Farther North, I see islands which belong to Canada. To the West I see the Saanich Peninsula and to the southwest I imagine I can see Victoria. Farther South and West, I see the Olympic Peninsula with its vast wilderness area.

To the south, I look down and see freshwater lakes nestling quietly in deep canyons, surrounded by rich green forest. Farther south I see Lopez Island, Whidbey Island and even farther South, I'm sure I see Everett, Washington. (Hah, I can even hardly see Lopez Island, but my imagination is running wild.)

I look East, and I can see Bellingham. Looming up behind Bellingham is Mt. Baker at 10,776 feet with its glacier covered peak. Looking back to the coast I see some little gray lumps. Yes, that is Chuckanut Drive.

All around the island, we can see ferries moving from one island to another. We are so high up, they look like toy boats.

As we stand there, the cool mountain breezes gently brush against us, cooling us against the hot sun which, by now is beaming down through clouds that float slowly overhead. Now I know why Jon had smiled when we were on Chuckanut Drive. This is a most beautiful place.

We leave Mt. Constitution and drive slowly back down the mountain taking in the fresh mountain air scented by the pine and fir forest. We turn at the road to Rosario Resort and drive through thick woods with wildflowers growing beside the road. At last we come to a large opening, and there before us, is Rosario's.

It is a very large and beautiful mansion that sits overlooking a deep blue cove, surrounded by evergreen trees. In the far distance are even more islands. The resort is in a protected cove that is halfway up the East leg of Orcas leading to Eastsound.

Jon and I walk into the marina and have breakfast. We have a table overlooking sail boats, power cruisers and outboard skiffs. After a wonderful breakfast we walk around the estate and pick up some of the history of Rosario's or as some people refer to it, the "San Simeon of the Northwest."

Rosario's was named after Rosario Strait. It was built by Robert Moran, (Remember Moran State Park) a pioneer of Seattle, who had become an industrialist in shipbuilding and who, at the age of forty-nine, was told he would die in two years. So he sold everything and moved to Orcas Island to live out his remaining years.

But, he lived thirty-nine more years. During that time, he built a mansion, dams, roads, steel and concrete bridges, a mill and even a large ocean-going sailing vessel. (Only to sail it for twenty miles, dock it, never to use it again.) Rosario's has a very interesting history.

As we walk back to Mabel, we become aware of the crowd she had gathered while we were away. These are people from another generation. Some of them look like they have been retired for a long time. We answer more questions as we prepare for the drive back to the ferry landing. As Jon starts Mabel, the crowd smiles at the sound she makes. Jon hits the throttle a couple of times and then lets the exhaust cascade back to a quiet rumble. There are a lot of Ohs and Ahs.

Jon wheels Mabel down the drive and up through the woods as the crowd we leave behind fantasizes about riding away in a maroon chariot into the sunset toward eternal peace and tranquility.

We drive slowly back toward Eastsound somewhat saddened, knowing our stay on Orcas Island is coming to an end. There is no teary mist streaming in the wind, but the sights are somewhat blurred.

We stop at an auto supply store and Jon buys a new blinker relay for Mabel. He replaces the old relay with the new one. The new one works, and we have turn signals again.

12 – Clark's Voyage to Canada

After we arrived in Sedro-Woolley it wasn't very long before I saw that Everett and Jon were going to be busy tending to Mabel and visiting with his mom. It was time for me to set out on my own.

I threw a leg over MoonShadow and took off South for Bellevue to visit with some of my friends that had migrated here from California a year earlier.

The trip to Bellevue was easy. It was all I-5 freeway. If you've seen one freeway you've pretty much seen them all.

However, on the way down my curiosity got the better of me. I had read about the famous Ballard Locks, a major engineering project that allows boats and fish to travel back and forth between the fresh water of Lake Washington and the salt water of Puget Sound. I managed to find my way off the freeway and with help I was able to see the Ballard Locks.[35]There was a tugboat pulling a large raft of logs through the locks. What I had heard was true; the locks are an impressive sight.

I visited with my friends and then decided that I wanted to stay in Anacortes so I could do some more exploring. I left that evening and drove back up I-5. I had to go through some significant rainstorms on my way to Anacortes. This was the only rain I was to encounter on my trip through the northwest and I'm glad. Driving through the rain on a motorcycle is not a lot of fun. However, thanks to MoonShadow's sure footedness, I made it to Anacortes and found a motel to stay the night.

The next day, I got up early and having heard of the natural beauty of the area, I decided to tour Whidbey Island from Deception Pass down to the southern end and back to Anacortes.

My first stop was at Deception Pass.[36] To me the name is somewhat misleading. Deception Pass is actually a huge cut between two cliffs with a sharp rock island in the middle of the gap. The cliffs are on separate islands, Fidalgo to the north and Whidbey to the south. The bridge that connects the two is quite dramatic as it is a long way down to the ocean water below.

---

[35] For more on the locks, visit

https://www.atlasobscura.com/places/hiram-m-chittenden-locks

[36] Visit https://parks.state.wa.us/497/Deception-Pass

In case you haven't already heard the story of how the Pass got its name, it was discovered by Capt. Vancouver and one of his sailing masters, Joseph Whidbey in 1792. The pass was named 'Deception' because Capt. Vancouver thought he and Whidbey had been deceived into thinking the island he named for Whidbey was actually a peninsula. Whidbey's discovery of the pass revealed that it was really an island.

Whatever the early explorers thought of it, it is a beautiful and impressive sight when you drive a motorcycle over it. From the bridge looking West you can see right out through the strait of Juan de Fuca to the Pacific Ocean. To the east lie the beautiful lowlands of the Skagit valley where they grow all those tulips. Farther east, looming above the Skagit Valley, are the beautiful Cascade Mountains.

Driving South through Whidbey Island I am struck by the diversity of scenery. I encounter everything from deep forests to open grassland and rolling hills, the island has everything except tall mountains.

I pass through the little towns of Oak Harbor, Coupeville, Freeland and finally reach Clinton on the far southern end of the island. On the way back I pass through Langley, which is a little quaint village full of arts and crafts, sitting on the east side of the island looking across the sound toward the Cascade Mountain range. It has beautiful vistas and looks like a place I would like to explore further when I have the time.

Taking my time, I ride back up to the north end of the island, over the Deception Pass bridge and back to Anacortes. It was a great day ride as Whidbey is about 55 miles long and gives ample time for sightseeing. I stay overnight and get up early next morning to catch the ferry to Orcas. I ride down to the ferry dock and just as we are to board the ferry, who should walk up behind me but Everett. He, Jon and Mabel had just arrived. It was great to be together again for our voyage to Orcas.

===================== ==================

While on Orcas, Everett was tired and had to take an afternoon nap. Jon was busy involved with his 'Quest for Tires' and Carolyn had to work. With nothing to do, I decided to explore. Orcas is a fascinating island that I cannot begin to describe in the little space I have.

But one thing I must mention is Mount Constitution. MoonShadow and I took a ride over to the East end of the island and up the long, twisty road to the top of the mountain. We discovered a fabulous view there. It was a truly inspirational experience. Even MoonShadow was excited about it as you can see here.

Finally, with our time to stay on Orcas coming to a close, I had not seen some of the Canadian sights I had my heart set on, so I made sure I got back to the Landing in time to catch the Ferry to Sidney, British Columbia.

The ferry leaves Orcas and stops at Friday Harbor[37] on its way to Sidney on Vancouver Island.[38] Friday Harbor on San Juan Island is the last stop in the USA before crossing the border so you must be sure to have your passports in order. During the ride the ferry glides between some of the most beautiful islands in the world. Finally we pull into Sidney and disembark through Customs. There is hardly any delay at all.

From there, I ride from Sidney to Victoria, and encounter a deer along the way. I had stopped by the roadside to consult my map when I get this feeling I am being watched. I look around and there he is about

---

[37] Visit https://www.fridayharbor.com/

[38] Visit http://www.sidney.ca/

twenty feet away in a thicket of trees and underbrush. It looks like Canada has some truly curious deer.

I stop at a local mom and pop general store for a soda and talk to the local people. I find they are very friendly, and they help me find my way down the island toward Victoria.

I have to hurry because I am on a fairly tight schedule. I want to get to Victoria in time to see the city before my ferry leaves for the US. Since my ferry is scheduled to leave at 4P.M., I haven't much time.

Luckily I make it to Victoria[39] in time to see its famous inner harbor. I am amazed at the architecture and cleanliness of the city. The Capitol building is an amazing example of ornate old-world styling.

---

[39] For more, visit https://www.victoria.ca/index.html#

Also impressive are the flowers and decorations all around the inner city and the harbor. I ride around the harbor, soaking in the sights. Another amazing sight is the famous Empress Hotel. I understand they have a very famous 'High Tea' that people come from thousands of miles away to enjoy. If it is anything like the exterior of the hotel, it must be truly something.

Before I know it, it is time to get in line for my ferry. I find the depot and park in the waiting line.

While I am there I observe two people in line in front of me. It is a guy and girl on a full dress Harley going through customs. The officials are examining them very thoroughly.

It seems to me that they take everything on that Harley apart down to the last nut and bolt. Whew, I'm wondering if they do this to all motorcyclists?

I am nervous when the customs official comes up to me. He asks me where I came from so I give him a thumbnail description of our trip so far. All of it, from California all the way up the eastern side of the Cascades, across the Northern State pass and through the San Juan Islands right up to my being here in Victoria.

He then asks if I have any guns or cigarettes. I say yes, I have some cigarettes in my boot and does he want to see them? I think, "Uh Oh, I'm in for it now." However, He just asks me a couple more quick questions and passes me. I am still wondering what the Harley people did to deserve such a detailed search when it comes time to get loaded on the ferry.

And, speaking of ferries, this ferry is nothing like the one I had come over from Orcas on. It looks like an ocean-going ship. In the front, a large door is cut into the front, near the Bow and the cars and bikes are being loaded through that door. Then it is closed tight. Inside, I lock up Moonshadow and tie him down solidly, making sure he is in gear. I don't want him to roll off his side stand during the crossing. That done, I head topside.

The ferry trip to Port Angeles is nothing like the voyage between the islands. First it takes us some time to clear Victoria's harbor. I had no idea we were so far inland. After we leave the inner harbor, it looks like we are crossing an ocean. There is land both far ahead and behind us but on either side, the ocean goes clear out to the horizon. It is a truly impressive ride that takes over an hour and a half to cross.

Once we land in Port Angeles, I have supper and talk to a couple of the local people about the bridge that crosses over from Washington to Astoria, Oregon. I am trying to decide whether to travel down the West or East side of the Peninsula. One local guy says that the bridge is bad for vans and motorcycles in bad weather. That decides it for me. I don't want to tempt fate again.

However, he also tells me of a spectacular sight that isn't too far from Port Angeles. So I ride out on a little inland side trip to a place called Hurricane Ridge.

It is well worth it. Looking North, back off the ridge I can see Port Angeles, the Strait of Juan De Fuca and clear across to Victoria, BC. It is something.

But if I look south I can also see the Olympic Mountain wilderness. The sight of this vast wilderness is breathtaking, for, as far as the eye can see, are forested and snow-capped mountains completely untouched by civilization.

The only way you can go into this wilderness is by foot or on horseback. It's just the way it was before the white man discovered America. It makes me feel good to be a mountain man, someone who lives in the mountains and loves this wilderness beauty. It is with some reluctance, I start back down from Hurricane Ridge.[40]

I leave Port Angles and ride down the western or coastal side of the peninsula on US 101 to the Aberdeen and Hoquiam area. It is a nice, less than four hour, 190 mile ride that takes me past fantastic cliffs, ocean vistas and the fabled Hoh rainforest.

At this time of year, there is no real indication of rain or the fact that the Hoh rainforest gets over 12 *feet* (144 inches) of rain per year. The whole trip down the Olympic Peninsula[41]is great. It is one great beautiful wild forested area. I feel right at home.

When I reach Aberdeen-Hoquiam, I follow the road back over to I-5 and then down the freeway to Portland.

Portland is a letdown. Always too much traffic and freeways. I catch up to Ev and Jon at the all British Car show. As I've always liked British cars, I enjoy the car show immensely.

=================== ===================

I take one last side trip to Fort Clatsop to see where Lewis Clark's expedition spent the winter before returning home. I find the tour of the reconstructed fort fascinating. I go through replicas of the very cabins they

---

[40]Visit www.outdoorplaces.com/Destination/secret/hurricane_ridge/

[41] Visit https://olympicpeninsula.org/

used through the winter in 1805-6. The importance of these explorer Heroes to US history cannot be underestimated. Prior to their expedition there had been no American claim to the Pacific Northwest. I leave humbled and appreciative of their achievements.

I get back on Moonshadow and ride a little farther down the Oregon coast highway. There are many beautiful sights along this road that goes all the way from the Washington border to the California border. Unfortunately I don't have time to see them all so I point Moonshadow eastward and cross over back onto I-5. Hours later, I meet Mabel, Jon and Ev on their way south.

We are together once again for the last leg of our journey, a drive that turns out to be our greatest adventure yet.

13 – Go South Young Man

At Friday noon, Jon and I leave Orcas Island. As I watch the foaming wake boil out of the ferry's stern, I fantasize about jumping into the blue water and swimming back to shore, hoping the ferry will never return so I can live there forever.

The ferry brings us into the Anacortes landing and we drive onto Fidalgo Island. The road leads south to the famous Deception Pass Bridge, one of the most beautiful and spectacular areas in the U.S. Jon points to a beach where he and Bonnie had picnicked so long ago. It is a wonderful place to walk on the beach or breathe in the scenery. A spectacular bridge connects Fidalgo with Whidbey Island.

A few miles of driving on Whidbey Island finds us at Oak Harbor. Dutch architecture and windmills are the theme here. I look to see a dike. I know I'll see a young boy with a finger plugging a hole in it. No such luck. No dikes.

The next town on Whidbey Island is Coupeville. If you amble down Coupeville's Front Street and stop at the Block House, you can see the Indian War Canoes.

We continue south on Whidbey Island, driving through more forest. In many places the land is open and neat little farms and ranches populate the island. Whidbey is a long island, the second longest in the US.

As we drive on, we see signs that lead you to other historical sites, old forts. For a hundred years, this area had many coastal defense installations guarding Puget Sound's entrance. Some of these are wonderful for tourists, like Fort Casey.

Fort Casey[42] was part of a three fort defense against attack from the sea. Begun in 1897 it was in use up through the Second World War. During WWII it used the latest technology in coastal defense, 10 inch Naval cannons on disappearing carriages. The guns would pop up over their defensive wall to fire at the enemy and then drop back down out of sight. Today, you can see examples of these impressive old guns on their carriages when you tour the fort.

The road ends at the southern end of the island at a Ferry Landing where we quickly catch a ferry over to the mainland at Mukilteo.

---

[42] Visit https://www.whidbeyislandbandb.com/visiting-whidbey/#7 for more information about Whidbey Island and its attractions.

I will never get tired of ferries. What a wonderful way to travel.

Jon and I make a quick stop at Don and Kathleen's house, and are surprised to see Kathleen up and around. In fact she and Don are packing their motor home for a trip into the Cascades for a short vacation. We are both happy to see her well on the road to recovery.

We leave for Snohomish on a second attempt to visit Jon's other sister, Judy. As we enter the freeway, I stick my head around the windshield to get a breath of air and promptly lose my hat. It sails like a Frisbee to the side of the road. We left it there. My gift to the Great Northwest. (Anyway, the bill was already flattened and it had a tire track across the top.)

This time, Judy is home. We meet her and her son Shane. However, we can only stay a very short time as we have a long way to go. Soon we are on the road to Portland. Our schedule is for Mabel to have her 'official' car show debut there tomorrow.

We get back on I-5 and head south, easily keeping up with the very fast traffic. To the South, far in the distance we can see Mt. Rainier. It must be 50 miles away and it is seen easily, even from way up here.

We stop at a truck stop for an early supper. As we leave the truck stop, I settle back in the seat and go to sleep, leaving Jon to drive. I awake in darkness and it takes a minute or two to orient myself. I notice the gas gauge is getting low and I mention it to Jon. He replies that he is running low on purpose and not to worry. After a while he finally pulls off into a station.

As we are getting gas a young man comes over to Jon and starts talking. I think it is another curious admirer of Mabel, but then he and Jon walk over to an MG parked next to the station. Oh, I think, he wants to brag about his car. After a while Jon returns, chuckling under his breath. It turns out that the young man is having trouble with his sports car and has asked Jon if he can diagnosis his problem.

It seems that at high speed the car feels like a vibrator and at low speed the car's rear-end wants to jump up into the air. Jon is chuckling because he had found the problem immediately and it really impressed the guy. Jon figured the young man would probably think he was a genius and remember the event for a long time. He didn't tell the fellow that we'd had the same problem on our trip to the Northwest. (What the heck, even I knew what was wrong.)

The darkness complicates things when we pull into Portland. Our plans are very sketchy. We stop at a Denny's, park under a street light and look at our maps and information pamphlets.

A friend of mine, Wally, had sent us a packet of information about the *All British Field Meet*. The paperwork directs us to the Red Lion Inn in downtown Portland. When we arrive there we discover that a bunch of rooms had been set aside for participants in the next day's events. They also had arranged guards for the autos.

Hearing this, Jon immediately responds, "OK! This is it. We stay here!" Alright, if he insists.

Before we know it we have a room and are standing on a twelfth-floor balcony overlooking downtown Portland. It is a really beautiful sight.

We are so impressed with the city's lights at night that Jon tries to take a timed exposure of it, bracing his camera on the windowsill. It is a nice try but it doesn't work. The picture turns out like some type of psychedelic color mess.

I call Wally, who lives 15 miles outside of Portland. He tells me we can prepare Mabel for the show at his house the next morning.

Jon goes downstairs to a meeting of the event committee where he retrieves a show package. It consists of a dash plaque, entry forms and cards which need to be filled out. The cards are to be displayed on the windshield at the meet. Using a felt tip pen, I put down

Mabel's vital statistics in the appropriate 'Olde English' Script.

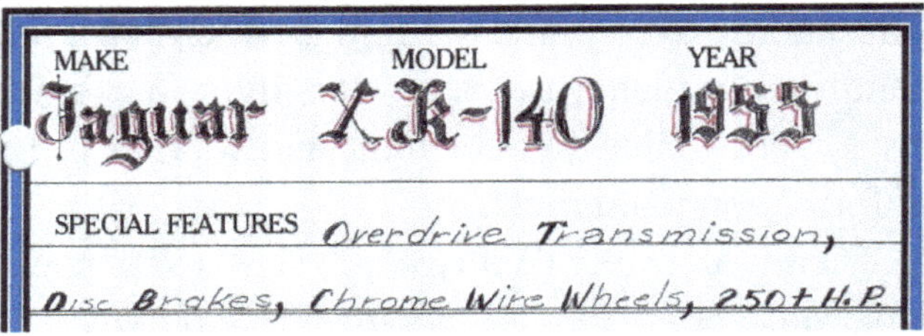

Afterwards, we get cleaned up and go to the bar for a couple of drinks.

The hotel night club turns out to be very lively. There is a small stage where four young people are wailing away on their instruments and singing to beat the band. They are having quite a good time up there. And we are having a good time watching them.

It's really late when we finally give up on the night club and hit the hay.

It has been a long drive from Orcas Island and tomorrow is going to take a lot of extra energy.

14 – Pride in the Park

Saturday, and another day begins early. It's hard to believe that we've only been gone a week. Our usual lives back in California are a distant memory. So far, this has been *some vacation.*

At 6:00 a.m. we start to move and grumble. Or did I really get up singing and dancing, full of pep and energy? Jon says I did, but I don't really remember. [Jon: He really did.]

We arrive at Wally's and meet his wife Bonnie and their children. We scrub and polish Mabel while Wally and his family give us encouragement. They seem to like Mabel. (Why not, almost everyone else likes her.) When we finish, we all stand back and admire how nice Mabel looks.

We figure we have done a pretty good job considering what little time we have and the fact that we are in the middle of a several thousand-mile cross-country trip. Even the two black wall tires on the rear don't look too bad. We say our goodbyes to Wally and family and we are off to the Portland International Raceway for the Field Meet.

We arrive on time and, before we have a chance to think, are directed right to our show spot. This show is well organized. We get Mabel settled down in her place, ready to show. We put the card in the windshield and look around.

Everywhere, we see people shining, polishing and cleaning everything in sight on their cars. We looked at Mabel. Hmmm, maybe we better start shining, polishing and cleaning too.

I get under the hood and wipe everything down. (It was like we hadn't even worked on it at Wally's. I didn't think we'd have to do this again.)

After about an hour, I am standing back taking a last look when I hear a voice behind me.

"She looks real sharp, but does she go?"

I turn around and it is Clark. Wow, he made it. We talk, Clark takes some pictures of Mabel and then he and I head off to see the rest of the show. This is a big show with all kinds of British vehicles well represented.

I take extra time going over the Land Rovers. Some of them have built-in camping equipment that is very well designed. We find a beer dispenser and a large shade tree and I spend a lot of time there. (Yes, it has gotten hot again.)

Meanwhile, Jon is busy showing Mabel. You can tell he is very tense. It's a good thing we have a beer and a shade tree to relax under. We're not tense at all.

As a side note, all our work cleaning and polishing Mabel was worthwhile because, Mabel, bless her little heart, took a Third in Class. That is quite an accomplishment considering the competition, our mishaps while touring cross country and the limited time we had to prepare her. After all, she is a 'driver' not a show girl. I am very happy for Jon. I am also a little proud of her and my work in helping her shine.

Due to the heat, Clark wants to leave the show early and says he will meet us down the road some place. That sounds a little vague because there is a lot of "down the road" ahead of us. I wonder where or when we will see him again.

I literally have to drag Jon out of the show and back onto the road. Jon is having a great time and just wants to stay and stay. Jon has spent so much time with Mabel, that he hasn't really had much time to see the rest of the beautiful cars in the show. However, since we only have one more day and a lot of traveling left to do, Jon sees my point and gives up on being able to be at the show for another several hours and look at the other cars.

It is early afternoon when we bid Portland and the All British Field Meet goodbye. It is time to head south again. There are still more adventures to be met and conquered.

15 – A Boring Road and a Hot Day

The drive on I-5 south from Portland turned out to be boring, boring, boring. It is straight freeway, the traffic is constant, the weather is hot and rest stops are far between. We try to contact Clark on the CB from time to time. At first we have no success. Finally, he answers. That's a nice surprise. He says he is following behind us about a quarter of a mile. After about a half hour he is travelling with us again.

The day is getting hotter. The road seems so very long, and I'm getting very grumpy. I am hot. I am thirsty. I am cramped. I need a break.

I yell, "Pit stop."

"Right on," Jon agrees. (Good thing. He'd better!)

We stop at some little place out in the flat land of Oregon's Willamette Valley, rest awhile and talk. It really does the trick. When we get back on the road, I feel much better. It is now really quite nice.

About 5 P.M. we arrive in Eugene, Oregon.[43] We stop at a bakery shop where an old friend works, but Linda is not there. Her partner is and we get some of their natural, home-made cookies. We then drive to the outskirts of Eugene, and stop at Linda's mother's house.

---

[43] Visit http://www.el.com/to/eugene/

It is so good to see Patty again. Good old PBRN (It's our nickname for her ever since we knew each other years before in California.). We sit in the shade sharing hugs, kisses and more hugs and have one hell of a good time visiting and reminiscing.

However, as much as we would like to, we can't stay more than an hour or two. Before we know it, our time is up and off we go again, heading south.

The road through the valley is finally coming to the hilly area that marks the beginning of the Siskiyou Mountains in southern Oregon.

We arrive at Roseburg, Oregon.[44] We see the Garden Villa Motel by the freeway and it has a pool. That is IT. That's as far as we are going today. We check in for the night. In five minutes I am in the pool. It is difficult to leave the pool because I just want to float around and let the water drain off the heat.

As I enjoy the refreshing water, my mind jumps from one thought to another. Then, it zeroes in on Mabel's

---

[44] Visit http://www.el.com/to/Roseburg/

troubles. Or, the lack of them. Why, we'd not had a bit of trouble since we left Orcas and headed home. I wonder why?

Then, I remembered a horse that I rode once. Going out on any ride she limped, coughed, and sweated like crazy. You'd have thought she was going to die. But, when you turned her toward home, she would suddenly come alive, like she was ready for the Kentucky Derby. They call a horse with that characteristic, Barn Sour.

Had Mabel gotten "Barn Sour?"

I mentally reviewed her problems. Well, to be fair, her being run out of breath and getting lathered up wasn't her fault. Jon made some mistakes in restoring her. And you couldn't really blame her for the tires failing, those were more age related. (My bad maneuvering couldn't have had anything to do with that…naw.) Still, she had eaten her generator, gotten sea sick and lost her direction but Jon was able to fix those problems quite handily.

It wasn't like she was doing all this herself. It was more like we had been on a lengthy shakedown cruise— like we used to do in the Navy. And now that we have all the bugs out, the trip home is turning out to be really quite uneventful…so far.

After a few hours in the pool, we walk over to a local restaurant. We are all hungry. Jon orders the prime rib. With that, he has a large baked potato with plenty of sour cream, butter and chives. His vegetables are cucumbers, sour cream, minced green onion and lemon juice all mixed together and chilled. It looks delicious.

I have grilled Coriander Chicken. It has been marinated in soy sauce, ground coriander, brown sugar, pepper corns and garlic. A slice of Rice Indene complements the dish. For a vegetable I have a striped tomato. A peeled tomato that has 5 deep parallel cuts is placed on a curl of iceberg lettuce. Cottage cheese seasoned with chives is placed between each cut. The top is dusted with paprika. Oh, so good.

We wash our dinner down with a good wine from a local winery.

You guessed it, Clark orders a hot dog. A sweet and sour relish mixed with catsup is ladled over the half-cooked frank. The stale bun crumbles as Clark shovels his dinner to his open mouth.

Jon and I just shrug. We've come to accept our friend's terrible taste in food—as a matter of self-preservation—if nothing else.

Later, Clark and I are staying up, watching TV.

We are watching something on the news about large forest fires in the Sierras and Northern California when Jon climbs out of his bed and hits the remote control that turns the TV off. He falls back into bed and then starts groping for the light switch, finding it he turns off the light.

Amazed, Clark and I are left sitting in the dark. In his polite, gentle way, Jon has told us that we are going to sleep.

Now!

16 – Trial by Fire

Next morning after breakfast, we leave Roseburg behind and head south. The scenery is beautiful, and the ride is uneventful. I realize that heading home is not nearly as exciting as heading out on an adventure. I glance in the rear-view mirror and see Clark on Moonshadow, 25 yards back. The road finally lulls me into a long nap.

We pull off the freeway at Grants Pass where we find a coffee shop. Clark talks about taking the coast route home. To do that he would have to travel highway 199 (the Redwood highway) over to the coast at Crescent City, South to Eureka on US 101 and then catch Highway 299 to come back East to

Weaverville. Jon and I are going to continue on I-5. Clark estimates the coast route mileage and then I-5's mileage to Redding and then home.

Jon mentions the news we've been hearing about the fires in Northern California and wonders if they will present any problem. Clark decides to check on that. He gets up and goes over to the phone and calls the Highway information service. Moments later he comes back to our booth.

"Well, guys I guess I'm going on I-5 too. According to the CHP there are several forest fires blocking highway 299 just west of Weaverville."

"Really? When did that happen?" I ask.

"I guess the ones we heard about when we left California are still burning. In fact, they've gotten worse." Clark replies.

"But we left over a week ago." Jon puts in. "You mean they're still burning?"

Clark's gave his typically long-winded answer, "Yep."

"Did they say anything about I-5?" I want to know,

"Well the CHP said something about haze, smoke and some brushfires nearby. They have travel advisories posted, but so far it's not closed like 299. It's funny," he mused, "I never heard of a fire blocking that highway before."

Although this raises our concerns, Jon and I are happy we'll have a few more miles with our good buddy.

Together, we leave the restaurant and start up our vehicles.

Leaving Grants Pass, the road begins climbing up through steeper and steeper mountain passes. All goes normally for a while. Then, a few miles after leaving Medford we notice smoke in the distance, beyond the mountain tops. Even way up here, it must be coming from those forest fires we've been hearing about. That is an ominous indication.

Like the fires in the high Sierras, a set of serious summer forest fires had been raging around I-5 when we departed last week. Because we had detoured off I-5 at Redding and gone to Weaverville, we had skirted around them. So we hadn't seen anything of them when we came north. But now, unknown to us, we are headed into the exact region where they are burning...furiously.

Started by Lightning strikes, during a very dry summer, the first area heavily hit was a very popular vacation spot, Yosemite National Park. Soon thousands of fires were blazing all over Central and Northern California and southern Oregon. These fires raged out of control for *months*. This series of fires have gone down in history as the famous "Fire Siege of 1987."

This series of forest fires are now burning over 300 thousand acres of forest, creating millions of dollars of damage, causing thousands to be evacuated and many people to lose their homes and their lives. Firefighters are being called in to fight them from all over the USA.

What we don't know at this time is there are now over one thousand fires burning in northern California in the Trinity-Alps and Klamath National Forest. A state of emergency has been called for this unusually large series of fires. We don't realize the situation is serious at all, until we see the smoke. The fires now are directly in front of us.

As we drive farther south, the smoke becomes thicker. It continues to thicken and spread until, gradually, it covers the whole sky. It is getting so thick it is beginning to block out the sun. As the sun fades, the world around us is turning orange and grey. Now the sun is just an orange glowing circle in an orange brown, smoky sky.

"Clark, are you ok?" I radio our buddy on his bike just behind us.

"So far." Comes over the CB. "I am keeping my head down below my windshield. I can still breathe. It's not burning my eyes yet. But it sure smells bad."

"We're smelling it too. It smells like burned cedar and fir trees." I shoot back. "Jon, I'll see if I can get some news or information on the radio." Jon nods his head and keeps peering through the smoke, his eyes glued to the road.

I turn on Mabel's radio and scan the local stations. The FM band is silent. We're too far up in the mountains to pick up any FM stations. I try the AM band. At last I stumble onto a local news reporter.

"…We have reports that the fires are threatening many small towns along I-5, Highway 299 and the surrounding area. In the small town of Hyampom, just west of Weaverville, over three thousand firefighters are fighting a life and death struggle to save the town. Weaverville itself is also being threatened by several fires surrounding it in the nearby mountains. We understand the forest service cannot use aircraft to bomb the blazes because of the smoke. We will keep you advised as we get more information…"

I turn to Jon. "Should I tell Clark about Weaverville being surrounded by fires?"

"Ev, Clark has a radio too. I'm sure he knows. If anything, he'll probably want to get home so he can volunteer to fight the fire and save the town." Jon is still fully concentrating on finding the road through the smoke and haze.

What we just heard brings fresh worries. The fires have created an inversion layer that prevents the smoke from blowing away. The smoke has become a major problem in fighting these fires. This is also what is causing the sky to darken and the sun to glow orange. The smoke and low visibility are preventing the forest service from using the usual aircraft technique of bombing the fires with retardant. Right now, in the middle of the day, firefighters are being forced to use flashlights or their fire truck headlights to read their maps because the smoke is so bad.[45]

Jon also turns on Mabel's headlights. It is strange to be driving down the freeway in the middle of the

---

[45] Referenced: LA Times "Smoke Thwarts Air Battle Against State's Worst Fire" September 08, 1987" MARK STEIN and IMBERT MATTHEE, Staff Writers

afternoon with the headlights on, but we need them. I look back and Moonshadow's headlight is on also. Even so, it's hard to see the road ahead.

"Hey guys, I think this is getting worse. Look up ahead." Clark's voice comes across the CB. "Are those fires I'm seeing alongside the road?"

I look up. I'm startled to see several small fires on both sides of the road. In the distance, farther away from the interstate are a whole line of fires. Ahead of us, I can see even more. Hey, this is getting serious.

"Yes, I see them, Clark," I nervously reply.

I turn to Jon. "Jon, what should we do? We're in an open roadster and on a motorcycle. None of us have any fire protection at all. Are we going to try and drive through a raging forest fire?"

"Stay cool, Ev," Jon shoots back. "I certainly don't want to stop here. The road is still open so far and there aren't any fires on it…yet. Anyway, as long as Mabel keeps running I think we can make it through."

"…as long as Mabel keeps running?"

Did he really say that? Oh. Dear. I can't help but flash back to all the times we've had trouble already. Oh Dear. More Trouble? I hope not!

Silently I say a little prayer. I pat Mabel's side. "Come on Mabel baby, don't fail us now. You're not going to get mad at me because of that little crack I made about you being barn sour, are you?" I don't quite whisper that last thought.

Almost at the same second that thought crossed my mind, I heard Mabel's exhaust note, cough.

"What was that?" My ears shot up and my eyes jerked open wide.

"That's funny." Jon was looking at the instrument panel. "I thought I heard Mabel misfire. Hmmm, she seems ok now."

"Does she do that often?" I try to sound nonchalant, but my heart rate has already shot up enormously.

"No hardly ever." Jon pats the dash. "I'm sure you're going to be just fine...aren't you, Mabel dear?"

Mabel doesn't say anything. Her growling engine note is steady now as we speed down the highway. I relax a little. Jon's soothing tone seems to help.

The fires are getting closer. Small brush fires are now flickering on both sides of the highway. Are they getting more numerous? It...it looks like they are. They are!

This isn't something you read in the newspaper or see on the news. This isn't happening somewhere else, this is happening now, to *us*. As we drive onwards through the smoke and haze, there are fires just off the roadside to our right and left. I see sparks are starting to fly up in the air over us.

Then I notice another thing. There is no traffic on the road . . .in *either* direction.

"Uh, Jon, do you see any traffic?" You couldn't cut through my anxiety with a chain saw! "You don't suppose they've shut down the freeway, do you?"

"God, I sure hope not." Jon's reply is not very reassuring. "I haven't seen any signs or signals yet. But, also, I haven't seen any exits for several miles, have you? There's nowhere we could turn around right now anyway."

"No," I admit. Still my mind jumps frantically from one possibility to another. What should we do? Should we keep trying to make a fast run for it through all these fires? Should we turn back after coming this far? Will we have to stop, join the firefighters in fighting these forest fires? Will we become roast toasties?? (Ok, I know, I know, now I'm getting a little hysterical.)

We can clearly see the local fires are out of control, plainly threatening I-5 and surrounding areas. Could it be they're shutting down I-5 right now and we don't know it yet?

We drive on, Mabel droning with her normal, steady growl. With every mile the fires, the smoke and the haze seem to be getting thicker and thicker.

The conversation between Clark, Jon and me dwindles. Our happy traveling vacation attitude has literally gone up in smoke. It's not knowing what lies ahead that is getting to us, including this inferno that is raging dangerously all around us right now. At least Mabel is growling right along.

Then, suddenly, Mabel's engine falls silent. We're slowing down!

"What's happening?" I scream at Jon.

"I think we have a problem." Comes back Jon's tense voice.

This is no time to have engine trouble. I glance at the fires all around us. "Jon, do something. If we stop here, we're gonna die." Yes, I am now officially *hysterical*.

"You're right, Ev. It's time for immediate action, *Spread your legs!*"

"*WHAT?!?*"

"You heard me." With one arm, on the steering wheel, Jon is fumbling behind the passenger's seat with the other. He pulls his arm out. He raises it high over my head. *He's holding the biggest hammer I've ever seen!*

"Do it, NOW! Quick, *spread your legs!"*

Never argue with a man with a giant hammer in his hand. I quickly spread my knees wide.

BAM! BAM! BAM! Jon's hammer strikes the floorboards directly between my feet.

Cough…POW! GRROWLRROWLRRRR… Mabel is suddenly alive again. Wow! Gasp! Phew!

Jon is calmly returning his hammer behind the seat.

Clark's voice comes over the CB, "Hey, Mabel's shootin' at me. What's going on?"

"Yes, my question exactly." I'm still shocked at what just happened.

Jon picks up the CB mike and looks at me. "Clark, don't worry, Mabel must have gotten some debris in her fuel that last stop. The diaphragm in her fuel pump got stuck and I had to unstick it. Just stay to one side in case it happens again."

"You mean that's what you were doing with the hammer? Where the heck is the fuel pump, anyway?" I'm still shook up.

"You're sitting on it." Jon explains calmly. "This rarely happens. Well, except on the rare occasion Mabel doesn't like a particular girl I'm dating. She'll intentionally stick her fuel pump like that and make me bang her floorboard to get her re-started. Naturally that girl will never ride with me again. It's really embarrassing. You can't believe how many girls she's run off. Sometimes I think she's jealous."

"Really?" It sounds like he's pulling my leg.

"Yea." He sighs, "My first XK-120 was like that too. All Jags have feline personalities. They can get very protective of their men. But, this time, I think Mabel just had something caught in her 'throat.' At least, I hope that's what it was."

As we fly down the highway between the flaming brush fires, I fervently hope he's right. I reflect that there is more to owning a classic sports car than I ever realized.

Grimly we press on through the cinders and smoke, steadily, determinedly.

Mabel's got her second wind now. She's running like she is also frightened by the fires surrounding us. I reflect that neither jungle cats nor humans like being burned alive.

The flickering fires, smoke and brown haze remind us of the danger we are in as we continue racing southward through this strange world.

Clark is worried that he may not be able to get home. And, if he does, he may not have a home left. Jon and I also worry about getting through, back to the Bay Area. If we can, at least our homes will still be there.

What seems like hours pass. I can only sit and worry while we fly along. Jon's face stays pressed up to the windshield. Mabel's growl pours out behind us as we push onward through miles of brush fire populated, smoky, grey-red-and-orange, world.

Then, unexpectedly, Clark's voice comes through the CB.

"Hey guys, maybe my eyes are deceiving me but I think the smoke is starting to fade up ahead."

"Are you sure? I don't see any change."

"I think so. I've been watching and it looks like I can see farther."

Is it true? Is Clark right? Are we saved? Straining my eyes off the side of the road through the fires into the trees, it looks like we might be.

"Yes, I think you're right. I send back, "I think the roadside fires become less numerous too."

Slowly, up ahead a hole in the smoke definitely seems to be opening. There the sky is definitely getting brighter. I think I see a tiny bit of clear sky.

"Hurray!" I shout spontaneously and hear two other echoing voices, "Yahoo!" that's Jon… and "EEHAA" coming from Clark. Mable doesn't say anything. She just keeps steadily growling onward. Bless her soul.

Finally.

Gradually we are coming out of the danger area and into a clear sky with a hot sun. A very bright sun. I had forgotten what a blue sky and a bright sun looked like.

We are happy our encounter with this historic catastrophe seems over. Never would we have expected, nor would we have ever wanted, the adventure of being caught in the middle of "The Fire Siege of 1987."

17 – A Surprise and Farewell

Once again the highway is back to being long and straight. After another few hours of travel, the fires we've just escaped are becoming only a vivid memory. All the tension drains from me, my eye lids become heavy, my body relaxes, a great calm comes over me and I slowly drift off. Sleep? Boy, do I sleep.

I am having a nice dream, and something wakes me up.

"What's up?"

It's Jon. "We're pulling into Redding. It's time for fresh gas and food. You want something to eat?"

"Sure." I pick up the CB mike and speak to Clark "Food, food, food."

I hear back, "Good, good, good."

We pull in and stop at a Carl's Coffee Shop. Jon and I get out and stretch while Clark slides slowly off Moonshadow. A lot of yawns. It's been a dramatic, tense and tiring time on the road today. More than we expected or ever want to do ever again.

We drag ourselves into the restaurant and sit down.

The waitress comes up to us, "What'll ya have?"

"Could we see a menu?" Jon asks.

"It's on the sign over the counter, bub." The waitress responds with a swish of her hips and a slight sneer.

I look above the counter and see a list of items.

Let see, the Number One is Soup of the Day. The Number Two is Chef's Surprise. I skip that one real quick. It's usually just leftovers in a soup. I know that trick. Let's see, Number Three is a Chile Dog and Number Four is a Chicken Salad Sandwich.

I stop there and tell the waitress, "I'll have the Number Three."

Jon said, "I'll take the Number Four."

"I'll have Number Two." Clark adds.

I start to tell him what the Chef's Surprise usually is, but I stop myself. I think, "What the heck, let him learn a little. Besides, with what his choices in cuisine have been, he won't be offended by whatever they serve him." I grin inwardly.

My Number Three is a Chile dog smothered with onions, mustard and walnuts. Not bad, but not great.

I look over at Jon's plate. He has what looks like a piece of dehydrated chicken on day-old bread. What looks like thick chicken soup has been poured over the top. Yuk...that's not a winner either.

The first thing they bring Clark is Blue Point Oysters on the half shell, chilled on a bed of ice, and a small bowl of fresh boiled shrimp, still in the shell.

What! Jon and I look at each other in amazement.

When he finishes that he is served a Lobster Newburg, double-baked potato and an Italian salad. His dessert is a Mocha Soufflé.

Astonished, I looked at the sign above the counter again. Jon looks at me, speechless.

Since we are finished with our lunch, I ask Clark, "So, how was it?"

He responds "Well, I believe the sauce on the Newburg was just a little thick. On the Italian salad, the green beans could have been fresher. Just a little soft. A little bit more sour cream and green onions in the double baked potato would have been nice. Now the Soufflé, ahhh; that was perfect."

Both Jon and I are shocked speechless.

Finally, I get up the courage to ask, "You kind of lucked out, getting a meal like that didn't you?" I still do not believe it.

"Well, to tell you the truth, an old girl friend told me that if I was ever in Redding and ate at Carl's Coffee Shop, to be sure and order the Number Two Chef's Special."

I take out my black book and carefully write "Redding - Carl's Coffee Shop - Number two."

Jon pays the bill and leaves a two penny tip. Obviously, he isn't as happy as Clark. As Jon and Clark walk away, I take one of the pennies.

At long last, the time has come for us to part. There is some small talk between us. We are avoiding the subject about splitting up. We try to hang on just a little longer. We have been through a lot in a short time. It is amazing how something as simple as a shared road trip can change one's feelings toward others. It is a happy but in some ways, a sad time for all of us.

Clark and I shake hands, but it doesn't seem enough. So, we give each other a big hug.

Clark climbs on Moonshadow and heads west toward Weaverville. He's anxious to get home…and we don't blame him.

We climb in Mabel and head south for the Bay Area.

As we leave Redding, Jon picks up the CB and calls Clark. A goodbye over the CB. Clark responds one last time.

From then on, the CB sits silent. Hauntingly quiet. I keep waiting for Clark's voice. I check out the rear-view mirror, trying to catch a glimpse of the Honda. For days he's always been there …now, he's not there. Neither he nor his voice are ever there again.

On through the long hot San Joaquin valley we drive. Hours float by. Mabel is humming along like the contented cat she is.

The heat makes the landscape shimmer. It's shimmering so much it blurs.

Finally, we arrive in the Bay area around 5 p.m. A quick trip back over the Bay Bridge—it looks different now—and down Bayshore freeway to Belmont. We arrive at my apartment around 6:00 p.m.

Jon steers Mabel over to the curb and parks. He pulls on the emergency brake, reaches up, and turns off the ignition. Mabel's deep melodic song is stilled. For the first time in over a week, she really is quiet…and so are we.

We sit and listen to the quiet. We don't talk. I think of the past nine days. In that short time we've gone over 2,700 miles—almost far enough to cross the whole country from Coast to Coast—and we've had countless surprises, discoveries and adventures. Our trip is over. It is now in our memories, forever. After all the years of talking, planning; after all the weeks of preparation, and after these last nine adventurous days, we have done it. And it was far more than I ever imagined it would be.

There were so many good times. Memories of Clark, Jon and Mabel; of Diablo Dam Resort, Ferries, Orcas Island, Everett, Washington, the high mountain passes, the wide-open prairies, the beautiful islands. They will stay with me forever.

And I will never forget the intensity of our many close calls; my almost getting us killed passing a motor home, our breaking down in the middle of nowhere and our good luck in surviving the Fire Siege of 1987. Yes, this adventure will be with me always.

After a few minutes, I turn and grasp Jon's hand.

"Thanks, my friend. Thank you so much".

He helps me unload my gear.

Mabel raps her pipes as Jon starts her engine. He turns, waves, and together, they disappear down the street.

I stand and listen to that rumbling melody until it fades away and there is quiet.

Good bye Jon.
Good bye Mabel.

And thank you.

THE END

Everett L. Jennings

I ask you, who would learn of a famous local Sports Car Rally and decide to compete by entering a 52 passenger Greyhound Bus?  Well it turned out to be a Silicon Valley Rally they'll never forget when the "Rubber Duck, Rally, Racing and Fun team crossed the finish line and fifty people piled out of the bus and started to dance around the finish line. Everett Jennings had not only completed the rally, he had brought the party with him.  Everett was that kind of person; innovative, entertaining, and funny. He was a big guy with a big personality and a great big smile who brought happiness to a lot of people. Of all the souls I have met in this life, his was the most uniquely upbeat. Whereever he is today, there will be laughter and happiness.

Everett L. Jennings July 31, 1938 - July 24, 2016

Clark Baldwin

Who was the first to show me that, just because you're born into a life, doesn't mean you can't break out of it, and be free. I wish others would learn from his example. Clark is great with his hands, and deep with his thoughts. Living in the fast lane of Silicon Valley society did not fit his ideal so he packed up and  moved to where he could live life on his own terms. Combining a love of hot rods, antiques and the high mountains makes for a unique lifestyle, but he combines them with class. Clark's life shows that we are captains of our own destiny if we but take the helm and sail toward it.

Now, that is a self-made man.

Jon C. Rogers

From a paper boy to a Spacecraft Engineer; from a library page to a National Land Speed Record holder on Motorcycles; from a truck driver to one of the nations renowned Spaceship Archeologists, Jon's varied life and number of careers almost defy definition. There is much more to tell about Jon's endeavors and his voyage through life. That information can be found on his website at www.joncharlesrogers.com.

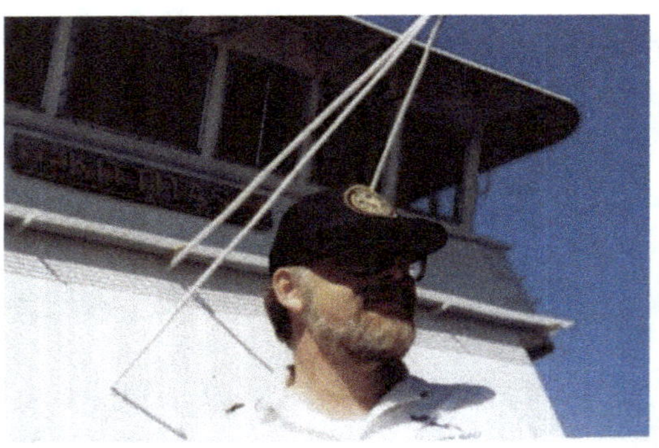

As a final note, Jon promised Everett that he would finish Everett's story of their great odyssey together regardless of the consequences. Having done so, he hopes that you have enjoyed the journey.

Mabel

This story wasn't the end of Mable's travels. Jon corrected her problems and in the following decades, Mabel made multiple trouble-free trips between California and Washington where she now lives.

Today, she rests cozily in her own personal, heated garage and enjoys going on occasional sightseeing trips through the beauty of Western Washington during sunny weather.

Although she's decades older, she hasn't aged a bit.

Oh, and in case you're wondering; her 'gold' headlight rims aren't custom; they're original.

During her restoration, Jon discovered Jaguar made them from solid brass and they were so beautiful polished, he's been polishing them ever since.

He says they add to her unique charm.